GW00499509

AN
ACCOUNT
of the
MINING DISTRICT
of
ALSTON MOOR
WEARDALE and TEESDALE

THOMAS SOPWITH

Davis Books

First published
1833

This edition 1984

Reprinted 1989

Davis Books Ltd
140, Westgate Road
Newcastle upon Tyne

ISBN 0 946865 02 7

Printed & Bound by
Smith Settle
Otley Mills, Ilkley Road
Otley, West Yorks.

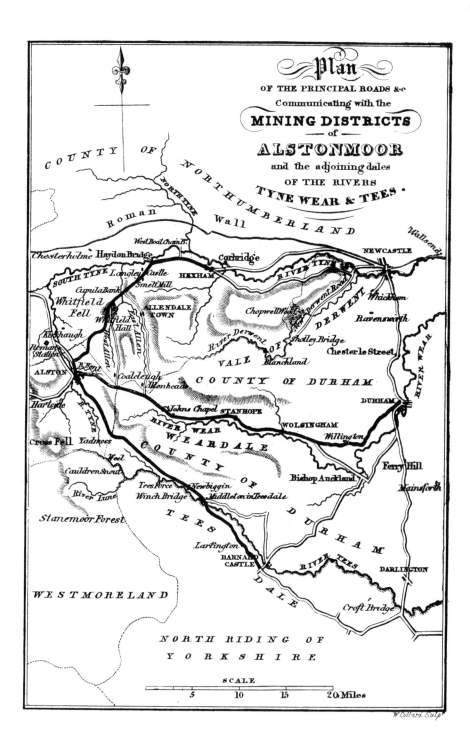

AN ACCOUNT

OF THE

MINING DISTRICTS

OF

ALSTON MOOR,

WEARDALE, AND TEESDALE,

IN

Cumberland and Durham;

COMPRISING

DESCRIPTIVE SKETCHES

OF THE

SCENERY, ANTIQUITIES, GEOLOGY,

AND

MINING OPERATIONS,

IN THE UPPER DALES OF THE RIVERS

TYNE, WEAR, AND TEES.

BY T. SOPWITH,

LAND AND MINE SURVEYOR.

ALNWICK:

PRINTED BY AND FOR W. DAVISON.

SOLD ALSO BY THE BOOKSELLERS IN NORTHUMBER-
LAND, DURHAM, CUMBERLAND, &c.

MDCCCXXXIII.

PREFACE.

THE Lead-Mining Districts of the north of England comprise an extensive range of highly picturesque scenery, which is rendered still more interesting by numerous objects which claim the attention of the antiquary, the geologist, and the mineralogist, and, in short, of all who delight in the combined attractions of nature, science, and art. Of these districts no detailed account has been given to the public; and a familiar description of the northern lead-mines, in which so many persons in this part of the kingdom are concerned, has long been a desideratum in local literature. The present volume aspires not to the merit of supplying this want; but, by descriptive notices of the principal objects of attraction, is intended to convey some general ideas of the nature of the lead-mining districts, and to afford some information which may serve as a guide to those who visit them. The red lines on the small frontispiece map denote the routes, which are more particularly described. These are, from Hexham to Alston, both in the vale of TYNE; from Alston down the TEES to Barnard-Castle, the first point where the dale is traversed by public conveyances; and from the city of Durham, the highest coaching place on the WEAR, to Alston. In these routes, which comprise in all a distance of about 100

miles (including the journey from Barnard-Castle to
Durham) the antiquary and architect may find the
following objects deserving of notice.

The venerable remains and beautiful architecture of
Hexham Abbey Church ;—the stately Castle of Langley, and the romantic fortalice of Staward Peel;—the
vast and exceedingly perfect remains of a Roman station covering nine acres of ground, and having the bold
contour of seven ditches in excellent preservation;—
the massive pavement of a long unbroken line of
Roman road ; — the stately ruins of Barnard-Castle in
Teesdale, and the more perfect castellated mansions of
Auckland, Durham, Brancepeth, and Stanhope, seated
in the mining dale of Wear ;—one of the finest English
Cathedrals, abounding in rich examples of the Norman
style, and numerous other architectural and antiquarian objects, which abound throughout these interesting
districts.

The geologist and mineralogist have ample stores
for inquiry and admiration, presented by the geological
structure and mineral treasures of the mining dales,
and the lover of landscape scenery will find a succession
of views which cannot fail to afford the liveliest gratification.   Among these may be briefly enumerated the
fine scenery of the Tyne above Hexham, and near
West-Boat Chain-bridge ; the romantic cliffs and woody
banks at Cupula and Whitfield ;—the magnificent prospects from Cross Fell and Hartside ;—the waterfalls
of Nentforce, Eshgill, Cauldron Snout, and Tees
Force ; — the scenery of Teesdale and Weardale,

abounding in the greatest variety of landscape views, from the wild and solitary mountains, whence the sister streams of Tees and Wear arise, to the more fertile and umbrageous lands through which they pass on their way to the German Ocean.

The machinery and curious processes used in preparing the ore for smelting, and the beautiful specimens of subterranean riches displayed in the shops of mineral dealers, all tend to combine the most rational enjoyment with the most agreeable exercise, and to fill up a succession of those intellectual treats which it is the object of the tourist to obtain.

This rapid sketch may evince, that the mining districts possess numerous sources of gratification to the inquiring traveller, and the author of these pages is convinced, from the opinion of highly intelligent persons who have visited Alston Moor and its vicinity, that it deserves more notice than it has hitherto received. The situation of this district renders it particularly suited for summer excursions. An easy and pleasant day's journey conducts the tourist from the heart of the mining districts to Newcastle, Durham, or Barnard-Castle on the one hand; or, on the other, to Carlisle, or Appleby, or to the far-famed and much-frequented Lakes of Cumberland. The readiness of access to most of the objects deserving attention, and the civility and intelligence of the inhabitants, together with the comfort of the inns, greatly enhance the pleasure of traversing this alpine range of country.

The following notices were chiefly collected in a
private diary kept by the author during a residence of
four years in Alston Moor, and have been arranged at
leisure times in their present form. The ascent of
Cross Fell and the visit to Ale-Burn Cavern are retained
in the narrative style in which they were written at
the time. The progress of the work (trifling as it is)
has been delayed by various causes, and the entire
manuscript is presented by the author to his much-
esteemed friend, the printer and publisher, who, with
more of admiration of the country it describes, than
any prospect of pecuniary recompense, offers it to the
public in its present shape.

                                              T. S.

Newcastle, May, 1833.

ERRATUM.—In page 25, line 22, for 12,000*l.* read 1200*l.*

CONTENTS.

INTRODUCTION.

General Situation and Extent of the Mining Districts.—Of the Penine Chain of Mountains, and of the principal Dales.—Characteristic Features of the Scenery.—Limit of Cultivation.—Rivers and Mountain Streams.—Hills.—Duration of Snow.—Storms.—Climate.—Roads, &c. 1

CHAP. I.
FROM HEXHAM TO ALSTON.

West-Boat Chain-Bridge.—Haydon Bridge.—Langley Castle.—Smelt Mills.—Staward Banks.—Whitfield.—Vale of South Tyne. 11

CHAP. II.
ALSTON MOOR.

History.—Royal Charters.*—Privileges of Royal Mines.—Decay of Forests, &c —Form and Extent of the Manor.—General Description.—Town of Alston.—Church.—Curious Inscription. 19

CHAP III.
TYNEHEAD, NENTFORCE LEVEL, &c.

Geological Phenomena.—Clargill Force.—Eshgill Force.—Waterfall.—Dimensions and Extent.—Nentforce Level.—Romantic Entrance.—Subterraneous Excursion in Boats, &c. 28

CHAP IV.
ROMAN STATION AT WHITLEY.

Walk by Tyne Side.—Bed of the River.—Randalholme Hall.—History, Antiquities, and Inscriptions of the Station.—Maiden Way, or Roman Military Road. . . . 33

CHAP. V.
CROSSFELL MOUNTAIN.

Ascent.—Prospect.—Sunrise.—Western Descent.—Dufton Pike, &c. 43

CHAP. VI.
HARTSIDE.

Prospect.—Comparison of other Mountain Views at Stirling, Edinburgh, Eildon Hills, and Cheviot.—Helm Wind, &c. 53

* Hodgson's Northumberland.

CHAP. VII.

Ale-Burn Cavern.—Hudgill-Burn Cavern, ... 64

CHAP. VIII.

GEOLOGY.

Comparative magnitude of the Earth, and its Strata.—Brief notice of Geological Theories.—Importance and interest of the Science.—Primary and Secondary Formations, &c. 76

CHAP. IX.

STRATA OF THE MINING DISTRICTS.

Familiar Illustration of the Arrangement of Strata.—Rise and Dip of Strata.—General Division of Strata.—Grindstone Sill.—Fell-top Limestone.—Coal.—Upper Coal Sill.—Upper and Lower Slate Sills.—Firestone Sill.—Pattinson's Sill.— Little Limestone.—Great Limestone.—Tuft.—Limestone Post.—Quarry Hazel.—Girdle or Till Bed.—Four-fathom Limestone. — Coal. — Nattrass Gill Hazel. — Three-yards Limestone.—Six-fathom Hazel.—Five-yards Limestone.— Slaty Hazel.—Scar Limestone.—Cockle-Shell Limestone.— Tyne-Bottom Plate.—Tyne-Bottom Limestone.—Whetstone Bed.—Great Whin Sill. 85

CHAP. X.

MINERAL VEINS.

Comparative Magnitude of Veins.—Various Names of Veins. —Prior Formation of Veins or Cross Veins.—Hade and Throw of Veins.—Contents of Mineral Veins.—Great Sulphur Vein.—Spar.—Galena.—Silver.—Copper.—Slip Vein.—Gash Vein.—Flats. 101

CHAP. XI.

LEAD MINES.

Progress of Mining.—Old Method of working Mines.—Nentforce Level.—Ventilation of Mines.—Discovery of Hudgill Burn Mine.—Present Mode of working Mines.—Mine Shops.—Visit to a Lead Mine. 116

TEESDALE.

Yadmoss.—Cauldron Snout.—Tees Force.—Winch Bridge.— Middleton in Teesdale.—Barnard-Castle. . . 143

WEARDALE.

Durham.—Cathedral.—Neville's Cross.—Brancepeth Castle.— Bishop-Auckland.—Stanhope.—Head of Weardale.—Nent Head.—Nent Hall.—Hudgill Burn.—East and West Allen. —Vale of Derwent, &c. 166

ACCOUNT

OF THE

MINING DISTRICTS, &c.

INTRODUCTION.

General Situation and Extent of the Mining Districts—Of the
Penine Chain of Mountains, and of the principal Dales—
Characteristic Features of the Scenery—Limit of Cultivation
—Rivers and Mountain Streams—Hills—Duration of Snow
—Storms—Climate—Roads, &c.

THOSE parts of England which adjoin the Scottish bor-
der possess many considerable attractions to interest
the stranger. Some of these have long been celebrated,
and much frequented by visitors from various parts of
the kingdom; while others have remained comparatively unknown. The stupendous barrier erected
across this portion of the island by the Romans, and
the numerous vestiges of antiquity scattered over the
northern counties, have been the subjects of much and
able illustration. Still more has the romantic and sublime scenery of the Lakes in Cumberland and Westmoreland attained a celebrity which justly renders the
tour of that district one of the most deserving objects of
the traveller's attention. Besides these, however, the
northern counties of England are distinguished by
another and very prominent range of scenery and remarkable objects, which, though scarcely at all known,

B

yet possess both importance and interest to render them deserving of attention. These are to be found in the lead-mining districts, which occupy the central portion of the island of Great Britain; and, from the gratification derived by many intelligent strangers who have visited them, it may be safely affirmed that they only require to be known, to be much more generally attended to than they have hitherto been.

The features of the scenery in these districts are alike removed from the rich luxuriance of the cultivated low lands of Great Britain, and from the alpine steepness and rugged grandeur of the mountains in the highlands of Scotland and in the vicinage of the Cumberland and Westmoreland Lakes. Those who have visited these celebrated resorts will at least in the mining districts find the charm of novelty, and enter on an entirely new scene of speculation and inquiry.

The principal portion of the mining districts in this part of the kingdom may be considered as extending about twenty miles from north to south, and the same distance from east to west. The square of 400 miles thus formed, and lying equally about the junction of the counties of Northumberland, Cumberland, Westmoreland, Durham, and Yorkshire, comprises the manor of Alston Moor—the mountain ridge of Crossfell, and the dales of the Tees, Wear, East and West Allen, and the Derwent. Besides the tract of country thus included, there are other extensive and important mining fields, which, being separated by tracts of cultivated land, cannot be considered as forming one district: these extend considerably into Yorkshire, and the other adjoining counties, in various detached parts of which mineral veins have been wrought: some of the principal of these will be afterwards noticed; but the scenery and characteristics of the mining districts now to be detailed must be considered as chiefly limited to that portion of them already alluded to.

A lofty range of mountainous moorlands stretches from the borders of Scotland, with little interruption, to Derbyshire. It has been variously called by different writers the Back-bone of England,—the English Appenines, &c. ; but the most appropriate name is that derived from a passage in Richard of Cirencester's description of the Roman state of Britain, " the Penine Chain." This range of hills attains considerable height at the King's Forest of Geltsdale, and Hartleyburn and Coanwood Commons, in Northumberland; from thence, stretching in a southern direction, it increases in wildness and sterility, attains its greatest elevation at the mountain of Crossfell in Cumberland, and continues in a direction nearly south-east, occupying a very considerable part of the district above mentioned. The average width of this portion of the Penine Chain may be considered as varying from 20 to 25 miles, but its extremes are in many places difficult to determine. The coach road from Hexham to Penrith enters it immediately after having passed Whitfield Hall in Northumberland, and crosses it obliquely for 20 miles to Melmerby in Cumberland.

The river Tees rises at the south end of the summit of Crossfell mountain. Four miles down this stream, and within a mile north of it, is the source of the South Tyne river, into which on one occasion the water of the Tees was conveyed for mining purposes. These rivers run in exactly opposite courses, so that, but for the intervening high land of Tynehead Common and Yadmoss, the vales of Tyne and Tees would be continuous in one line. About 10 miles east of the source of these rivers, the Wear and East and West Allen rivers have their rise ; the first running nearly parallel with the Tees, and the others with the Tyne, form the principal mining dales, and comprise the richest and most important part of the northern mining district.

The elevations of this part of the Penine Chain are not bold and rugged, but very high, massive, and rounded, rising, in most instances, gradually from the east and descending more steeply on the western side. In the numerous valleys which occur throughout, the cropping or bassett of the strata is very obvious, and affords peculiar facilities for geological research. The influence of calcareous strata on the soil is very conspicuous. The bassett of the great limestone, which is the thickest and nearly the highest calcareous stratum, forms, in many instances, the limit of cultivated land and of human habitations. Below it, the hill sides in spring and autumn present a beautiful green surface, and in summer an abundant and flowery produce in the meadows. While on the same hill above the limestone, bare short grass, ling, and moss impart the brown and dreary aspect which characterizes all the higher portion of the mining district, rendered, in moist weather or in winter, still more dreary by hanging mists on the summits, or wasting snows scattered over the wide expansive sides of the hills; but, from the massive character of the scenery, rendered beautiful and even sublime by the blue shades of evening, or the subdued effect of moonlight.

In the midst of these dales numerous streams of water are seen pursuing a somewhat rapid course over rocky beds or blocks of various kinds of stone; some of immense size tumbled from the scars above, and others which have been carried downward by violent floods. Their waters vary from the angry torrent rolling along with almost resistless force, to the gentle

stream which murmurs along its rocky channel or is
swallowed up in the fissures which frequently occur in
the limestone rocks, and these transitions, owing to the
extent and steepness of the hills, are often very sudden
A portion of the refuse excavations of the mines is
frequently carried down by the stream, and fills the
beds of the rivers with great variety of rocky and
mineral substances.

The average slope of the hills is from 8° to 10°.
Their summits, it has been stated, are, "for a great
part of the year, covered with snow ;" but this observation is too extended; the hills here, as in most other
countries where the mountains are not very high, retaining their wintry mantle only a few days longer
than the neighbouring valleys; and even the "alpine
snows" of Crossfell soon waste away to a few drifted
patches, which, on the approach of summer, become
very small, and usually disappear in May. In former
times, however, there is no doubt that both the quantity
and duration of snow were much greater than at present. In several instances, partial remains of snow
have been found on Crossfell at midsummer. In
the latter end of May, 1809, the weather was very fine
and warm; but on the last day of that month and on
the 1st of June, there fell a considerable quantity of
snow, accompanied with a strong wind; many sheep
were overblown on the moors, and the whole country
was covered several inches thick on level ground. As
it disappeared, the contrast of the snow and the
green pastures and hedges had a remarkable appearance ; but such exceptions have only occurred in
these elevated districts in common with other and
more favoured portions of the kingdom, increased,
in some degree, by the altitude of even the valleys, and
by the tempestuous influence of storms on the sum-

mits of the adjoining fells. Here the traveller or miner, who at such times had occasion to cross these high lands, was exposed without shelter to all the fury of the storm, and hence the name of Alston Moor (the principal mining manor in the district) has long been associated with an idea of extreme wildness and severity of climate. To this, the brief account of it appended in a note to Hutchinson's History of Northumberland has contributed. That historian unfortunately visited it in stormy weather, and so combines the howling of the winds, and the violence of the rains, with his notice of the country, that he scarcely leaves room for the supposition that it may appear to greater advantage in more favourable weather. The note alluded to has been transcribed into recent works, and contributes to the agreeable surprise of those who, judging from this source of information, expect in Alston Moor to find only a dreary wilderness and inclement storms.

As great severity of climate and prevalence of rainy weather are yet very generally considered among the characteristics of the mining districts, the following statement of the weather at Alston in 1825, founded on accurate observation, shows that the proportion of fair weather is not very widely different from less elevated countries. In that year, the respective varieties of weather may be classed as follows :—

	days.	days.
Very fine and sunny,	$107\frac{1}{3}$	
Fair but dull,	143	
		$250\frac{1}{3}$
Very wet,	$54\frac{2}{3}$	
Moderate rain,	$48\frac{2}{3}$	
Snow,	$11\frac{1}{3}$	$114\frac{2}{3}$
Balance of fair weather,		$135\frac{2}{3}$

The number of very fine days, sunny throughout, was 68; of fine days, little clouded and without rain, 96; of cloudy days with little or no rain, 71; of moderately rainy or snowy days, 52; of very stormy days, 24; and of days partly so, 54. The fairest months were March, July, and August; the most rainy were May, October, and November.

Situated, however, as these districts are, in the most elevated portion of one of the narrowest parts of the kingdom, the atmosphere is necessarily subject to considerable changes. On the dreary summits of the high fells, which abound in them, and which must in one direction or another be crossed to gain access to the inhabited valleys, the pitiless pelting of the storm often rages with a violence which those who have lived only in milder climes can scarcely appreciate. Being further distant from the sea, very sudden and heavy falls of rain occur less frequently than in the district of the Lakes, and in winter the quantity of snow, falling with a northeast wind, is frequently less than in the neighbourhood of Newcastle and the eastern coast of Northumberland, In summer the heat, powerfully reflected from the inclined surface of the hills, is sometimes very oppressive, and especially on those bare moors which afford no shelter from the scorching rays of a burning summer sun. Hence the traveller who in one month ranges over the fells with hands and face blistered with heat, may, a few months after, traverse them with eyelashes covered with icicles, and a mass of frozen snow and ice suspended from his horse's head. The inhabited parts of the mining districts are not, however, exposed to these violent extremes. The air is somewhat colder, and the weather, generally speaking, somewhat less mild and settled than the low lands on each side of the Penine Chain; but the difference is by no means so great as is commonly imagined. It may be observed, however, that, from the peculiar character of the scenery, rainy weather shrouds it with a very cheerless and uncomfortable aspect, while, on the contrary, in fine weather many of the valleys have a freshness and beauty that render them highly interesting, and agreeably surprise those who expect to find nothing but bare and dreary wastes.

The want of good or even of tolerable roads was for a long period the principal cause of the mining districts being so little known. About 50 years ago, scarcely a regularly formed road was to be found in them; goods were chiefly conveyed on horses or galloways, which followed the soundest track over the moors; the leading horse, having a bell attached to it, was called the bell-horse. The roads which have since been made have in many instances followed these tracks in the most inconvenient and circuitous directions. Some of these yet remain in use, and in several places present a steepness of ascent perfectly terrific to those unaccustomed to mountainous districts. The period is not far distant when carriages could not be brought into the interior vales, and it was so late as 1824, when Lord Lowther travelled from Alston to Teesdale, by Yadmoss, in the first carriage that had passed over that dreary and exposed fell, on which, some four hundred years ago, the Scottish army escaped from Edward III. then encamped in Weardale, by laying boughs to prevent their sinking in the moss. In addition to bad roads, the traveller on this and other adjoining fells had too often to encounter the bewildering effect of mist or snow storms, and very lamentable results in the loss of human life were till lately not unfrequent. In the course of the last six years a vast improvement has been made by the formation of new lines, and all the most interesting portions of the district are now traversed by roads which, for gradual ascents and smoothness of surface, are equal to any in the kingdom.

This improvement, which forms a new and important æra in the mining districts, has been chiefly effected under the auspices of the Commissioners of Greenwich Hospital. The personal inspection of their able secretary, Edward Hawke Locker, Esq., enabled him, in reporting on the hospital's estates in these parts, to point out the great advantages which would be derived from such an undertaking. The services of the celebrated Mr. MacAdam were put in requisition, and in the following four years considerable progress was made in constructing new, and improving portions of the old, lines of road. These together extend from Hexham to Penrith, from Brampton to Alston, and from thence by the vales of Nent and Tyne to Weardale and Teesdale; and they are so far completed as to afford safe and convenient facilities for travelling in all these directions. One of the first fruits of the greatly improved state of the roads was the establishment of a post coach, which commenced running between Hexham and Penrith, by way of Alston, where, on the 29th of September, 1828, a band of music and a large concourse of people assembled to witness the first public conveyance that had ever traversed this part of the country. In the following spring the proprietors introduced a new and elegant four-horse coach from Newcastle to Penrith, by which visitors have a pleasant and easy access to the mining districts, and considerable advantage is also afforded by the great saving of distance between these towns, instead of the former circuitous route by Carlisle.

The scenery throughout this line of road is fraught with objects of interest. In clear weather the delightful variety of the prospects between Newcastle and Hexham is truly enchanting, and to those who are not limited to time, the road on the south of the Tyne presents a succession of incomparably beautiful views; perhaps in no ride of equal extent is there a greater diversity of objects and different kinds of scenery than what is afforded by this journey. Even those who have not an opportunity of spending a few days in closer examination, cannot, when passing in fine weather, fail to be highly gratified with the singular and interesting objects which present themselves; and those who have leisure to visit them will find much that is worthy of attention. To direct the tourist, by presenting concise descriptions of the scenery and remarkable places of the mining districts, is the object of the present work.

CHAP. I.

FROM HEXHAM TO ALSTON.

West-Boat Chain-Bridge—Haydon Bridge—Langley Castle—Smelt
Mills—Staward Banks—Whitfield—Vale of South Tyne.

————

THIS is one of the most frequented approaches to the
mining districts, and possesses considerable attractions
not only in the hasty transit of a stage coach, but many
which well repay a more leisurely examination. The
town of Hexham contains little to occupy the attention of the tourist, except the remains of its venerable church. In the interior the transepts and
choir deserve examination, and present on a small
scale some of the finest characteristics of cathedral
architecture. The vicinity of Hexham is extremely
beautiful, and the views from the neighbouring eminences are fraught with variety and interest. The
group of old towers in the midst of the town, and the
luxuriant effect of the gardens which adorn it, render
Hexham very picturesque. Those who spend a little
time here will greatly enjoy the beautiful scenery of the Tyne, whose wide, smooth, and placid
surface for some distance above the bridge gives it,
especially at evening, much of the sublime effect of
lake scenery ; and this effect is still more observable
from the side of the river about a mile above the town.
A pleasant walk of another mile brings the tourist to
the Suspension Bridge at West Boat, erected in 1825-6
under the direction of Captain Brown, R. N., by whom

also the Union Suspension Bridge over the Tweed was projected. The piers of West-Boat Bridge are distant 313 feet 8 in. The deflection of catenary was intended to be 1 foot, but, owing to the chain yielding when the floor of the bridge was laid, it is now perfectly straight. The bridge is supported by four pair of chains, two on each side ; the links are 10 feet long, and from their junction depend iron rods which support the frame-work of the bridge floor, the construction of which may be seen by walking under the bridge. It contains about one-fourth part less timber and iron than the Union Bridge, and cost nearly 5000*l*. It is a curious and interesting object, and both it and the neighbouring scenery amply repay a visit.

From hence to Haydon Bridge is in fair weather a tolerably pleasant walk or ride, but without any re-markable objects to detain the traveller. The river Tyne is here crossed by a long and narrow bridge of six arches ; adjoining the inn, at the south end of which, are apartments for the use of the Receivers of Greenwich Hospital when they transact business rela-tive to the extensive estates in the vicinity belonging to that institution. The bank south of the inn has lately been ornamented by the erection of a long line of high wall with embrasures ; and on the same emi-nence are the Free School and Almshouses founded in 1685 by the Rev. John Shaftoe, A. M., Vicar of Ne-therwarden, who endowed them by deed of gift with his estate of Mouson, near Belford. This deed was afterwards confirmed in chancery, on account of a sub-sequent will, dated 1693. The estate then let for 80*l*. ; but upwards of forty years ago it had risen in value to more than 400*l*. per annum. Pursuant to the will of the donor, the trustees purchased a parcel of land on which they erected the school-rooms, with dwellings for the masters and ushers, and apartments for twenty alms-people ; the latter of whom are to be poor persons born in Haydon chapelry, and receive 2s. 6d. each weekly, and a supply of coals. The school is munificently endowed for the education of both sexes, under the superintendence of four teachers, but none can claim its benefits unless they reside in the chapelry of Haydon, or in the constablewick of Wood-Shields. There are generally about 140 boys and 90 girls receiving instruction at this large seminary. The head master must be of the degree of master of arts ; and, according to an act passed in 1819, he is to perform morning service every alternate Sunday at the chapel of ease. The trustees are empowered to raise or decrease the salaries of the teachers, but the master's is not to be less than 250l. per annum. The yearly stipend now paid to the others are, 64l. to the first usher; 63l. to the second usher ; and 30l. to the mistress ; besides which, each of the teachers has a house and garden.

On leaving this village, the route to Alston intersects a narrow and romantic valley, through which the road winds in a circuitous course; a wall of rocks on one side, and a very steep and high woody bank on the other, with a small stream between, have a romantic and secluded effect, oftener found in the deep and lone recesses of forest scenery than immediately adjoining a turnpike. Proceeding about two miles up this road the stately ruins of Langley Castle burst upon the view. This structure is one of the most perfect remains of its style of building in the county. The interior is 80 feet long and 24 wide ; at each corner is a strong square tower 66 feet high, and 14 feet square in the inside ; the walls are 7 feet thick, and the rooms arched with stone. Some of the buttresses are light and

C

elegant, the windows are larger than are commonly
found in ancient baronial edifices, and have some
remains of circular tracery and of small perpendicular mullions. A small door with a portcullis
on the east side leads to a circular staircase ;
the entrance to the hall or principal room from this
staircase is by a door with a pointed arch and ornamented capitals to the shafts which support it. The
foundation of Langley Castle is scarcely sunk below
the level of the ground, the interior is red with marks
of fire, and the whole of the stone is remarkably fresh.
This is the more surprising from the length of time it has
been a ruin. It is mentioned in 1542 as follows :—

" All the roofs and floors thereof be decayed, wasted,
and gone, and nothing remaining but only the walls ;
it stands in a very convenient place for the de-
fence of the incourses of the Scotts of Lyddesdale and
the *theves* of Tyndale, Gyllesland, and Bowcastle,
*when they ride to steal or spoil within the bishopric of
Durham.*"

This fine structure was formerly the capital seat of
the barony of Tyndale. It was held of the crown in
the time of King Henry I. by Adam de Tyndale, and
continued in his male descendants till the time of
Henry III. And hence by a succession of female
heirs it became the property of the Boltebys, Lucys,
Umfranville, and Percys ; it afterwards became the
property of the Radcliffes of Dilston, and was forfeited
in 1715 by James, the last Earl of Derwentwater. It
now belongs to Greenwich Hospital, and has by occasional repairs been kept carefully preserved.

About a mile from Langley Castle another very
curious and different scene is presented by the Smelt
Mills at Langley, belonging to Greenwich Hospital,
where the greater portion of the ore raised in Alston

Moor is converted into lead and silver. The buildings are numerous and extensive, and, from having been erected at different periods without any regular plan, have the appearance of a village. Leaving these on the left, the road continues by heathy moors and elevated bare land, and in two miles approaches the Allen at Staward. The romantic and picturesque banks of that river nearly covered with wood are then seen receding in beautiful perspective,—the rocky bed of the river, at a very considerable and nearly perpendicular depth below, and the ruins of Staward Castle above,—form a scene which never fails to excite the liveliest admiration, and far exceeds any encomiums that can be bestowed on it.

After passing along this lofty terrace, the road winds by a zigzag course down the almost precipitous and rocky face of Cupula Bank, and commands a fine view of the beautiful vale of Whitfield on the left, while, on the other hand, the wild and lofty rocks and hilly banks form a subject fit for the pencil of Salvator Rosa. A handsome stone bridge of three arches is here built over the united streams of East and West Allen. The bed of the river is formed by a stratum of limestone, supposed to be what in the mining districts is commonly called the Great Limestone ; and the steep scar of Cupula Bank presents the abrupt escarpment of alternating siliceous and argillaceous strata.

The ride through the vale of Whitfield is fraught with beautiful and highly romantic scenery. The retrospect of Cupula Bank is to the stranger a sight of wonder and amazement, forming so sudden and stupendous an obstacle to a direct line of road as is perhaps unequaled in these kingdoms. On each side of the West Allen river the banks are for the most part either fringed with natural copse wood or covered with plantations, the wide surface and verdant foliage of which sweetly adorn the narrow vale. The grouping of the scenery may be varied into the most beautiful combinations from several points of view, and especially from parts of the new road leading past Whitfield Church to Haltwhistle. The Church and Rectory House stand on elevated ground about half a mile from the road. The cemetery and gardens adjoining the house are laid out with great taste and judgment; the former being planted and the surface kept in excellent order, while the latter possess all the attractions that can be combined in so limited a space. These improvements have been chiefly effected by the Rev. Anthony Hedley, A. M., during his residence here in the absence of the Rev. T. H. Scott, Archdeacon of New South Wales, and Rector of Whitfield; and it may be added, that they are in unison with Mr. Hedley's zeal and attention in promoting the best interests of his parishioners, especially of the children, in the education of whom he has long exhibited an amiable and praise-worthy interest.

Blueback Inn, in the midst of the vale of Whitfield, is delightfully situated near a romantic bridge across the Allen, beyond which, its steep banks, with a winding road and still more winding footpath, are crowned by a large extent of beautiful plantations on the summit of the hill, and form an admirable subject for the pencil. A little further west, seated on a commanding terrace amid fine park scenery, but almost entirely concealed from the road by luxuriant foliage, is the mansion-house of William Ord, Esq., M. P. It was erected about forty years ago on the site of the ancient hall of the family of Whitfield; and for sequestered retirement and beauty of scenery is perhaps equal to any residence in the north of England. The vale

of West Allen, the broad surface of foliage of Monk-
wood, and the distant summits of the Penine Chain,
form interesting objects in the prospect from the Hall,
while in another direction the eye is delighted with
" the pomp of groves" that extend in a long and narrow vista, terminated by one of the neat little cottages
with which Mr. Ord has ornamented his estate, a scene
that cannot fail to excite many of the most pleasing
associations and poetical images of retirement and
peace.

Soon after passing Whitfield Hall, the traveller
enters on the range of hills, the general extent and direction of which have been already described.   The
road gradually ascends for several miles to the bleak
and lofty summit of Whitfield Fell, affording first a
panoramic view of nearly the whole course of the West
Allen river, and afterwards a more extended prospect
over the north-east part of Northumberland, bounded
by the hills of Cheviot, Hedgehope, of Rimside and
Simonside Moors, and in very clear weather the German Ocean may be clearly distinguished.   On reaching the top of the Fell, the mountain of Crossfell gradually unfolds its gigantic summit, stretching in a kind
of table land for nearly a mile in length; and proceeding further the whole ridge of this highest portion of
the Penine Chain appears.   Before commencing the
descent of the western part of the hill, a stone wall
forms the boundary of the county of Northumberland
and of the manor of Whitfield, and the traveller at
once enters into the county of Cumberland and the
manor of Alston Moor.

The vale of South Tyne here opens to the view, and
the features of the mining districts already alluded to
present themselves.   The houses scattered over the
lower parts of the hills are nearly all whitewashed, and

thus impart some liveliness to a scene in which wildness and sterility much prevail.   It has been justly
observed that the appearance of these districts is pecu-
liarly affected by different kinds of weather.   On a
fine sunny day most strangers are pleased and highly
interested by the prospects throughout this part of the
vale of South Tyne, while, on the contrary, a rainy
day, especially if accompanied with wind and hanging
mists on the fell, presents a spectacle of extreme
dreariness, which has contributed to the erroneous but
very prevailing idea of Alston Moor being a treeless,
miserable waste.   About a mile from Alston, the road
is carried along a terrace on the side of a steep hill,
and the extensive view from thence is much admired.
A nursery on the flat holmes near the river, and numerous plantations scattered along the sides of the vale,
present a much more beautiful scene than is usually
anticipated.   Lowbyer Inn adjoins the road about a
quarter of a mile from the town of Alston, and, as a
contrast to Hutchinson's description of an Alston Inn,
it is but justice to say that it has been much extolled
by noblemen, and other highly respectable individuals, as combining the pleasantness of a country
residence with the comfort and retirement of a " home."
The town also contains some good inns, of which the
Crown and Blue Bell are the principal.

CHAP. II.

ALSTON MOOR.

History—Royal Charters—Privileges of Royal Mines—Decay of Forests, &c.—Form and Extent of the Manor—General Description—Town of Alston—Church—Curious Inscription.

OF the early history of this important mining field, few materials have been collected. That it was occupied by the Romans is sufficiently testified by their works which yet remain in very perfect preservation, and from silver denarii having been found at Hallhill near the town of Alston. It is improbable that so extensive a work as the Maiden Way or great Military Road, constructed by that warlike people, would be prosecuted without discovering lead ore in some of the numerous veins which it crosses; and at the Roman station at Whitley in Northumberland, pieces of lead have been found as well as in numerous other places. In early periods the process of smelting ore was very simple. Piles of stones were placed in situations exposed to the west, which is here the most prevailing wind, and several places in the mining districts where these rude and imperfect furnaces were erected, retain the name of Boles or Bayle hills. That mining in this district is of great antiquity, appears from mention of several charters granted to the miners of " Alderston" nearly 600 years ago. They had royal protection granted in 1233, again in 1236, and again in 1237. In 1282 the king granted to Nicholas de Veteripont

(the original of the family name of Vipond) the manor
of Alderston to hold in fee of the King of Scotland, re-
serving to himself and the miners various privileges,
especially such as belonged to the franchise of Tindale,
within which Alston was then comprised.

At that period the aspect of the country must have
been widely different to what it now is, for many of
the dreary wastes which yet retain the name of Parks
and Forests were then covered with trees. The remains of these are often found in peat mosses, and the
miners who farmed their mines of the king, and
worked veins containing silver ore, claimed a right to
take any wood that should be near to, and convenient
for their said works, and also at their will and pleasure
use and dispose of such wood for burning and smelting,
for paying the workmen their wages, and to give to the
poor workmen of the mines.   These claims were, however, admitted by Henry de Whitby and Joan his wife,
who impleaded several of the miners for cutting down
and carrying away their trees; and further charged that
they had sold large quantities of wood from which the
king received no kind of benefit.   From the wood thus
sold, in addition to that used in the mines, which right
the miners stated they had exercised from time imme-
morial, it is obvious that these forests must have been
very extensive, and it furnishes some explanation of
the entire removal of these once beautiful adornments
of a hilly country.   On the other causes which have
contributed to the decay of forests on what are now
waste lands, some highly interesting observations have
been made in the writings of Sir Walter Scott.

King Edward III., in the seventh year of his reign,
confirmed several of these privileges to Robert, son of
Nicholas de Veteripont, and in the following year the
monetarii or coiners had their liberties confirmed by

the king; so that it appears Alston in these olden times had not only mines but a mint also.

In the 24th of the same reign the crown exemplified some charter of privileges formerly given to the Alston mines, and again in 1356 granted very large privileges to the same.

Henry V. let the manor and mines of Alston to William Stapleton, Esq., at an annual fee-farm rent of 10 marks, payable at the exchequer in Carlisle; and in the same reign the said William Stapleton and his tenants had their liberties and privileges confirmed to them for the said manor and mines.

The nature of mining was in those times very imperfectly understood. Science had not emerged from those visionary theories and idle speculations which so long cramped the energies of the human mind. As to Geology, it was alike unknown and unthought of, and it is highly amusing to take a retrospect of the whimsical notions which were gravely advanced and no doubt at that time implicitly received as profound wisdom. Thus in Sir John Petties' History, Laws, and Places of the chief Mines and Mineral Works in England, &c. (London, 1670), we find the following singular account of the formation of hills and valleys, and the use of the magical rod in discovering mines :—

" The usual method of historians is to begin with the creation, wherein I might tell you that when God breathed upon the face of the waters, that was a *putrifying* * breath, and that such waters as were *quiet* and *calm* turned into *plains or levelled earth*, and the *boisterous waters* into hills and mountains, according to the proportion of the *billows*, and their *spaces* into *valleys*, which have ever since continued in their wonderful

* Evidently an error of the press for *petrifying*.

and pleasant dimensions, the *seminal* virtues of all sub-lunary things being locked up and more durably preserved in them ; and yet from thence they are transmitted through *terrene pores*, either from their own *exhuberancies* or the *sun* or *stars extractions, into various and visible forms.*" " Such *superficial excrescencies* whether vegetable or minerals do direct the miners in their knowledge of the nature of the metals under them ; which *sometimes also is done* by the *virgula divina or magical rod*, being no other than a *hazel stick* cut in a *certain season of the stars' aspects*, still showing what *rare contiguity* there is between the stars, plants, animals, and minerals, as if they were but the *soft products* of those *meditullian putrifactions.*"

The same writer then proceeds to a somewhat forced interpretation of Adam's history, " of whom," he says, " I might tell you that he may be esteemed a *miner* from the text, where 'tis said that God placed him in paradise, and commanded him to *dig* or till the earth, as also a *refiner*, &c. &c." The work contains some curious information, from which the following extracts are made as illustrative of the state of mining at that period.

" The adit is from the Latin word *aditus*, that is to say, an entry, passage, or approach to a thing. And this is usually made on the side of the hill, but towards the bottom about 4, 5, or 6 feet high and 8 *feet wide* in the nature of an arch, sometimes cut in the rock, and sometimes supported with timber, so that the sole or bottom of this adit may answer the bottom of the shaft but somewhat lower, so that the water may have sufficient current to pass away, which is exactly known by the ordinary ways of dialling or the workman's keeping the water at his foot when there is any. And he is directed toward the shaft by a needle touched with a loadstone, the using whereof is called dialling, and by this and other arts the water is conveyed away with more ease and less charge than by pumps. And by these adits the fumes, damps, and unwholesome vapours are better dispersed, which otherwise might endanger the miners ; but if any of them be surprised with such a damp, so as for the present he may be deprived of his senses, he is drawn up out of the mine, and they dig a little hole in the earth, and lay him on his belly with his mouth to the fresh earth of that hole which speedily recovereth him."

The following particulars on royal mines at that period are interesting data in the history of mining.

" When the ore digged from any mine doth not yield, according to the rules of art, so much gold or silver as that the value thereof doth exceed the charge of refining and loss of the baser metal wherein it is contained, then it is called *poor ore* or a *poor mine.*"

" On the contrary, when the ore yields so much gold or silver as to exceed in value the charge of refining and loss of the baser metal in which it is contained, then it is called rich ore or a MINE ROYAL ; appertaining to the king by his prerogative, and herein consists the honesty of the refiner, for some have made very great products from that very ore from which less skilful essayers could extract nothing."

In the remainder of this, and in some other works, much curious information is afforded respecting the state of mining, and the various grants and immunities confirmed on mining adventures by the crown ; but these particulars are in a great measure too minute and technical to be generally interesting in the present work.

Alston afterwards became the property of the Hyltons, of Hylton Castle, in the county of Durham ; and in 1611 a considerable portion of the lower parts of the manor adjoining the rivers Tyne and Nent, was granted in leases for 999 years, by Henry Hylton, subject to the payment of certain annual rents which amounted to 64*l.*, but, with some encroachments taken off, are now 53*l.*, and a fine of twenty times the rent every 21 years.

The lead-mines, on a survey made about this time, were reported to be nearly exhausted, and in 1629 the whole manor,—including all the lord's rents and minerals, 120 acres of demesne land, with houses at Lowbyer and Mack Close, and a corn-mill at Alston,— was sold to Sir Edward Radcliffe for 2500*l.*, and remained in that family till the confiscation of the estates of James, Earl of Derwentwater, in 1716. It was granted by the crown, in 1734, to the Royal Hospital for Seamen, at Greenwich, and has since remained in the possession of the commissioners and governors in trust for that institution. Several other estates in the manor, and the adjoining manors of Whitley and Ale, have since been purchased in addition to this valuable property.

In form the manor of Alston Moor nearly resembles a square of about 6¾ miles, containing about 45 square miles or 29000 acres. It consists, as its name imports, chiefly of wild and barren land ; a considerable portion of the elevated land in it affording only subsistence for the hardier breeds of sheep, and an ample range for the sportsman. The division of common has in the course of the last twenty years greatly improved the appearance of the country, and in that period also several fine plantations have been reared, especially on the lands belonging to Greenwich Hospital. A narrow range of rich loam extends along the lower part of the valleys, producing luxuriant crops of fine meadow and rich pasture with some few sheltered patches of corn, the extensive growth of which is prevented by the climate. Numerous gardens and an extensive nursery furnish ample proofs of the fertility of the soil in the valleys, which, if intersected with hedges in the place of naked stone walls, or scattered over with hedge-row trees, would yield to few situations for picturesque beauty. Newshield Bank, on the east side of the Tyne, comparatively speaking, may in so bare a country be said to be extensively wooded; it has a fine appearance from some points of view, and the addition of a few belts of plantation on the opposite hills would be a very considerable addition to the general appearance of the country. As it is, some of the scenery which it affords is considered highly interesting by most strangers, especially when the blue shades of evening impress a character of sublimity on the surrounding hills.

This manor is described in one of Mr. Locker's reports, in 1821, as the most valuable and interesting part of the landed property of Greenwich Hospital. The mines then yielding an annual produce of 100,000*l.* and the lands producing a rental of about 12,000*l.* per annum. These latter are divided into small farms and allotments for the convenience of the miners, and are generally let to persons who obtain part of their livelihood by carrying ore from the mines to the smelting mills. In the same report Mr. Locker has sketched with spirit and fidelity an outline of the general character of the country and its inhabitants. " In reference to its population," he observes, " this manor is a highly interesting possession. The valley lies secluded from the rest of the country by the surrounding moors, and the inhabitants are an industrious and loyal people, moral and intelligent, and of simple habits. The nature of their occupation as miners leads

D

them to inquiries which greatly quicken their understanding, and urges them to seek from books such
parts of practical philosophy as are applicable to their
profession.   They are excited to industry by the prospect of independence, the successful adventures of
other miners acting as a powerful stimulus to the pursuit." This favourable testimony has been often confirmed by the observation of intelligent strangers, who
have been alike surprised and gratified by the well-in-
formed minds and plain but courteous behaviour of the
miners. The unassuming manners and great hospitality
of all classes in this and the neighbouring dales are
such as to call forth a high degree of respect and
esteem for the moral worth and social feelings which
accompany and direct them.

The town of Alston stands on the steep base of the
mountain of Middlefell, adjoining the confluence of the
rivers Tyne and Nent, which are both crossed by substantial stone bridges.   It contains about 400 houses,
and is on the whole rather meanly built.   The streets
are inconveniently steep and narrow.   A market-place
of triangular form in the midst of the town has an old
and somewhat clumsy cross in it; and the weekly
market on Saturday presents a scene of busy activity
not usual in country towns.   It has been proposed to
make a new market-place on the site of the Vicar's
Croft, a small field in the lower part of the town,
the completion of which, and the erection of some
buildings on a uniform plan, would greatly im-
prove the appearance of the place.   The church
is dedicated to St. Austin, and stands on a commanding
situation; it was erected in 1770, is a plain and neat
edifice, the interior remarkably so.   The tower contains a good clock and bell.   The latter was formerly
the dinner bell of Dilston Castle, and its sound can

scarcely fail to recall a melancholy remembrance of that unfortunate nobleman. In the church-yard is the following singular epitaph, erected at the expense of the sons of Crispin to commemorate an eccentric brother :—

> My cutting board's to pieces split,
> My size-stick will no measures meet,
> My rotten lasts turned into holes,
> My blunted knife cuts no more soles,
> My hammer's head is from the haft ;
> No more St. Mondays with the craft.
> My nippers, pincers, stirrup, and rag,
> And all my kit have got the bag,
> My lapstone's broke, my colors o'er,
> My gum-glass froze, my paste's no more,
> My heel's sewed on, my pegs are driven,
> I hope I'm in the road to heaven.

There are four meeting-houses in the town belonging to the Independents, Quakers, Methodists, and Primitive Methodists or Ranters ; a charity school supported by subscription, where 100 children are educated gratuitously ; an endowed grammar school, rebuilt in 1828, among the holiday sports of which in the olden time was that of a main of fighting cocks for a prayer-book at Easter. Some of the books thus won are yet in possession of some of the surviving scholars. A band of music, supported by public patronage, usually perform one or two evenings every week at Lowbyer Inn, or in fine weather make the neighbouring hills resound with melody.

CHAP. III.

Geological Phenomena—Clargill Force—Eshgill Force—Waterfall—Dimensions and Extent—Nentforce Level—Romantic
Entrance—Subterraneous Excursion in Boats, &c.

———

THE manor of Alston Moor contains also the popu-
lous villages of Garrigill and Nenthead. The former is
situated on the river Tyne, three and a half miles
above Alston, on the road to Tynehead, and is sometimes visited by persons wishful to see the source of
that river, which rises seven miles further south.
The stranger, by following the road through Garrigill,
will have no difficulty in finding guides to conduct
him to the place, near which also is a curious whin
dyke or wall 70 feet wide, thrown up through the
other secondary strata which form the bed of the river.
Near Tynehead Smelt-mill may be seen the great whin
sill or basaltic rock which underlays the Alston
Moor strata, and, if time permit, the stranger may
spend an hour in walking a short distance to Clargill
force, close to which a mineral vein has been partly
excavated and left in a condition which gives as
clear an idea of the nature of veins as can be seen
in the country. The bed of the rivulet, two or three
hundred yards lower down, presents a remarkably
clear view of various entrochi and other organic remains imbedded in a calcareous stratum, which is
locally called the cockle-shell limestone. In this

neighbourhood are the principal copper mines of the district, to which access may be had by applying to the agents, and some further notices of which will be introduced in describing the mines generally. About a quarter of a mile below Garrigill, a vein containing lead ore may be seen crossing the bed of the Tyne, and which has been worked to within a few feet of the surface. In this excursion up the Tyne, the rich lead mine of Holyfield may be visited. These objects, together with an excursion to Crossfell from Garrigill when the atmosphere is clear, furnish sufficient employment for one long and arduous summer's day, but would in most cases be better extended to two, in order to allow time for examination and inquiry. There are few to whom the inspection of such various and interesting scenes as are thus comprised would not prove highly gratifying:—the source of the principal river in the north of England—the geological interest of its vicinity—the curious and novel phenomena of the interior of lead and copper mines—the peculiar and characteristic scenery of the dale—and the magnificent prospect from the summit of Crossfell in clear weather, well repay the fatigue which attends mining and mountain excursions. To these may be added also the fine waterfall of Eshgill force, which, after heavy rains, is well deserving of a near inspection, but at other times the quantity of water is so inconsiderable that the general view of it from the road to Tynehead will be thought sufficient, and as it is mostly then that the weather is favourable for visiting Crossfell, any nearer approach to Eshgill would probably encroach on the time required for this extensive mountain ramble.

From the confluence of the rivers at Alston, the vale of Nent extends in an eastern direction for about five miles. This river, at a short distance from the town, and at only a few minutes' walk from Lowbyer Inn, falls over a precipice of limestone, which, though considerably worn by the water, is yet, and especially in wet weather, a fine waterfall, rendered more so by the romantic little valley which is formed by the precipitous escarpment of the rocks and woody banks adjoining. Large masses of limestone have fallen at different periods into the bed of the stream, over which the tremendous rushing of the great volume of water produced by heavy rains in so confined and rugged a channel, accompanied by the roar of the waterfall, form a terrible and sublime spectacle. On the south side of the outlet of this valley stands a large spinning factory worked by water brought from above the fall. Opposite to it is an assay office, in which the value and contents of the ores raised in the manor are ascertained, and near it is a depository for part of the ores either purchased by, or paid as duty to, Greenwich Hospital.

But the most interesting object in this place is the entrance to Nentforce Level, a stupendous aqueduct made by the Lords of the Manor for the discovery of mineral veins, and for draining the water from the mines above. This level was projected by Mr. Smeaton, the celebrated engineer, when one of the receivers of the Greenwich Hospital estates in 1775, was commenced in the following year, has been regularly prosecuted since that time, and is now carrying forward to the important mining field at Nenthead, the extent originally proposed. From the entrance already mentioned near Nentforce, it extends under the course of the river Nent for a distance of three and a quarter miles to Nentsbury engine shaft. Its dimensions are 9 feet in height and the same in width, but in many places, owing to the nature of the beds, it is considerably larger, and in a few places is so much as from 16 to 20 feet in height. It is navigated in boats 30 feet in length, which are propelled in four feet water by means of sticks projecting from the sides of the level; and thus may be enjoyed the singular novelty of sailing a few miles underground, and beholding with perfect safety the various rocks which it passes through, owing to the rise or inclination of the strata, and also the numerous mineral veins which it intersects. The hanging rocks suspended over the entrance with the romantic scenery adjoining, and the neighbouring waterfall, render a visit, even to the exterior, highly interesting; but this is much increased by a subterraneous excursion, which is frequently undertaken by strangers, and not unfrequently by parties of young persons resident in the neighbourhood. The old and often grotesque dresses worn on such occasions add to the mirth and cheerfulness which prevail—while the fine effect of vocal or instrumental music, and the exercise of propelling the boat, add to the singular feeling which is excited by the idea of so bold an adventure.

A voyage of about a mile in length, with the return, occupies as much time as will generally be devoted to such an excursion. More than this becomes tedious—the spirits flag, and the current of air, which is sometimes up the level, and sometimes down, might prove unpleasant by a longer stay. As a number of candles are usually taken up, a variety of beautiful effects may be produced by leaving short pieces of them burning at intervals; the reflection of them in the water presents a fine spectacle, and, by this means also, some idea is afforded of the vast extent of the level by the receding vista of lights. In the day-time the level

mouth is seen from upwards of a mile up the level; in
sunshine seeming like a brilliant star with radiat-
ing beams.   At such times also, the faint and
straggling day-beams which enter the level give to
the rugged outline and green mosses of the roof and
sides the same subdued but silvery brightness, which,
in immediate contrast with surrounding darkness, has
the same poetical character, the same inimitable effect,
as that with which the beautiful ruins of Melrose are
now for ever associated.

Such to the general observer is Nentforce Level.
To the geologist and the miner it possesses still more
and peculiar attractions; but these will be more appro-
priately introduced in a future part of the volume.
At present we proceed to notice such other objects in
the neighbourhood as are deserving of attention, and
possess general as well as local or scientific attractions.

CHAP. IV.

ROMAN STATION AT WHITLEY.

Walk by Tyne Side—Bed of the River—Randalholme Hall—History, Antiquities, and Inscriptions of the Station—Maiden Way, or Roman Military Way.

THE Roman station at Whitley, distant two miles from Alston, and lying near the turnpike leading from that town to Brampton, may be very soon and conveniently visited on horseback; but when time admits, and the river is not swollen, the walk to it from Alston or Lowbyer inn by Randalholme and Kirkhaugh is exceedingly pleasant; and varying the walk by returning on the opposite side of the Tyne is almost equally so. A footpath leads from Lowbyer inn past the old manor-house, and by stepping a short distance from it to the river side, may be seen the entrance of a horse level or adit driven for the discovery of veins. This situation also affords a view of the confluence of the rivers Tyne and Nent, and of the town of Alston. A few yards from the level mouth a mineral vein may be seen crossing a small syke; to strangers it is not very obvious, and may require to be pointed out. If any of the miners are present, the strangers' attention may be directed to an instance which here occurs of what is called the throw of veins—the limestone rock being several feet higher on one side of the vein than the other. But this and other similar details will be more fully explained afterwards.

The visitor may either return to the footpath, or pursue a briery but romantic walk along the edge

of the river, past a nursery belonging to Greenwich
Hospital, containing about seven acres of land, in
which the numerous plantations now rising in several
parts of the manor have been reared. This path
joins the former at a deep bathing place, called
the turnwheel, where the river sides are formed by
the same scar limestone stratum that Nentforce falls
over. The footpath continues through a few fields or
holmes, the luxuriant and flowery crops of meadow in
which, render them exceedingly beautiful in summer.
The adjoining banks are steep, for the greater part
covered with wood, and form a romantic amphitheatre, which has excited great admiration even in
travellers who have explored distant continents. Before
ascending the steep and woody bank through which
the footpath ascends, the lover of fine scenery or of
natural history will spend a little time on the banks
and rocky bed of the Tyne near this place. About
fifty yards lower down the stream, is a steep precipice
called Cats-Scar, and near it the scar limestone, on
which the river flows, is curiously worn into lozenge-
shaped prisms, traversing which may be seen a great
number of what are called, by some geologists, con-
temporaneous veins,—and which present in miniature
so many of the phenomena attendant on the important
mineral veins as to form, with a little explanation, an
interesting illustration, or rather elementary lesson, in
this department of geology.

From the top of Cats-Scar, is an interesting and
beautiful prospect of the Tyne and its curiously-fretted
channel below, of the hanging woods on the left, with
a full view of the town of Alston. Behind it rise
the extensive and dreary moors of Rodderup, and
beyond them the mountain of Crossfell rears its gigantic head.

An ancient peel-house, now white-washed, with an armorial escutcheon of stone on the north front, stands near the foot-path. This is Randalholme Hall, formerly the seat of the family of Randals, one of whom, William Randal Featherstonhaugh Ricardson Randal, is buried in the parish church. The estate has been recently purchased by the Commissioners and Governors of Greenwich Hospital. The substitution of a slated roof and gables in place of the old flat lead roof and battlements, and its occupation as a farm-house, have materially lessened the antiquity of its appearance, which well comported with its massive walls, some of which are upwards of seven feet in thickness.

On the north side of these premises a small bridge crosses Ale Burn, which here forms the boundary of Northumberland, and a pleasant woody road leads from hence by the east side of the Tyne to Kirkhaugh church. About a hundred yards above this humble edifice are stepping stones across the river, after passing which, a cart-road somewhat to the right leads through a few fields to the farm-house of Castlenook, so called from its contiguity to the Roman station, which lies toward the common, about a furlong south-west.

This interesting remain of antiquity is lozenge-shaped in form. The angles included by the sides are 65° and 120°, and the length of the sides on the summit of the station is 150 yards by 128 yards ; but the total area included by the escarpments and ditches amounts to nine acres. On the north are four, and on the west seven ditches in remarkably good preservation. The former extending in breadth from the summit of the station about 40 yards, and the latter 90. Still further north are the remains of the Hypocausta or baths—the supposed cemetery of the station—and, what is rather a variety in antiquarian researches, the perfect remains of a *Roman midden-stead*, which, strange as it may appear, has furnished many loads of excellent manure to the neighbouring fields, and been hitherto the productive mine of seve-ral interesting curiosities.

The history of the station is obscure. Mr. Horsley supposed it to be Alione garrisoned by the third cohort of the Nervii, but this opinion has been refuted, says Mr. Hodgson, by subsequent discoveries. Its former importance is however fully testified, as well by its extensive works as by the inscriptions and other vesti-ges of antiquity which have been found. Several of these are said to have been removed from the station about a century ago, and taken by Sir Thomas Robin-son to his seat at Rookby in Huntingdonshire. Among those that have been subsequently discovered, may be enumerated—

An altar found about twenty-five years ago in the cemetery, a few yards from the north-east corner of the station, with the following inscription :—

DEO
HERCVLI
C. VITELLIVS
ATTICIANVS
C. LEG. $\overline{\text{VI}}$
V. P. F.

The inscription on this altar may be read as follows :—

DEO HERCULI
CAIUS VITELLIUS
ATTICIANUS
CENTURIO LEGIONIS SEXTÆ
VICTRICIS PONENS FECIT,
Or, SEXTÆ VOTUM PERFICIENS FECIT.

Signifying that this altar was erected to the God
Hercules, by Caius Vitellius Atticianus.

On the right-hand corner of the inscription side of
the altar, a serpent is represented coiled round a tree,
and attacked by a rude figure intended to represent
Hercules with a club, which is cut on the adjoining
side of the altar. On the other side is a similar figure
representing the same deity strangling a serpent in
each hand. It was found fixed in a pedestal. On the
top is a square hole, in which it is probable a statue of
Hercules was fixed, as the head, a hand, and feet of a
colossal statue were found at the same time and place.
The head is yet preserved at the neighbouring farm-
house,—the altar was purchased for 7*l.* about ten years
ago, and taken to London.

Camden gives the following inscription found at this
station:—

IMP. CAES. LUCII SEPTIMI SEVERI ARA
BICI. ADIABENICI PARTHICI,
MAX. FIL. DIVI ANTONINI PII GERMANICI
SARMA. NEP. DIV. ANTONINI PII PRON
DIVI HADRIANI ABN DIVI TRAIANI
PARTH. ET DIVI NERVÆ ADNEPOTI
M. AVRELIO ANTONINO PIO
FEL. AVG. GERMANICO PONT. MAX.
TR. POT . . X . . IMP . . . . COS. IIII. P. P. . . .
PRO PIETATE AEDE . . . . VOTO . . . .
COMMUNI CYRANTE . . . .
. . . . LEGATO AVG.
PR. . . . . COH. III. NERVIO . . . .
RVM . . G. R. POS.

E

The original is probably destroyed. Mr. Horsley
gives the following reading of it from a copy which
he found at Appleby :—

IMPERATORIS CAESARIS LUCII *SEVERI* ARABICI
ADIABENICI *PARTHICI*
MAXIMI FILIO DIVI ANTONINI *PII*
SARMATICI NEPOTI DIVI ANTONINI PII PRONEPOTI
DIVI HADRIANI ABNEPOTI DIVI TRAJANI
PARTHICI ET DIVI NERVÆ ADNEPOTI
MARCO AURELIO ANTONINO PIO
FELICI AUGUSTO *GERMANICO PONTIFICI MAXIMO*
TRIBUNITIÆ POTESTATIS DECIMUM . . IMPERATORI
. . . . CONSULI QUARTUM PATRI PATRIAE
PRO PIETATE ÆDEM EX VOTO
COMMUNI CURANTI
LEGATO AUGUSTALI
COHORS TERTIA NERVIORUM
GENIO ROMÆ POSUIT.

Mr. Horsley found a fragment of an inscription
which referred to Caracalla, and there was, in his time,
a centurial stone here inscribed VEX. LEG. xx VV.
REFEC. And in the church-yard at Kirkhaugh an
altar dedicated DEAE MINERVAE ET HERCULI
VICTOR.

A small altar, on which are carved a patera and
urceolus, is fixed above the stable door at the east end
of the farm-house ; and a pegasus or winged horse,
rudely carved on a small stone, is built into the wall
of one of the outhouses.

About twenty-two years ago, the remains of a fine
sudatory were found at the north-east corner of the
station, out of which issues a clear and plentiful spring.

In 1810, Mr. Hodgson found many of the pillars of
the Hypocaustum standing covered with large thin
slabs of freestone and a strong calcareous cement, but
most of them have been removed at different times for

building materials, so that few vestiges of this part now remain.

In 1825, Mr. Henderson, the proprietor of the estate in which this part of the station is situated, in cutting a drain, discovered a large quantity of manure under a slight covering of soil, and, on trying a few experiments, found it useful as such, and laid considerable quantities on the adjoining land. In excavating it a number of curious remains were found, several of which are yet preserved at the farm-house. Among these were a great number of shoe-soles of various shapes and sizes; the larger one, now in Wallington Museum, measures $7\frac{1}{4}$ inches, and the other $5\frac{1}{4}$ inches in length. They are fastened by leather thongs and round-headed nails. A boot found at the same place is also preserved in the Museum at Wallington.

A copper breast-pin was found here, and is now in the possession of Wm. Crawhall, Esq., of Allenheads. A spoon, apparently of the same metal, was found in 1829.

Various fragments of earthen red tile, and of vessels of different kinds, have been found from time to time, many of them containing groups of horses and human figures in relief. Fragments also of leaden pipe, glass bottle necks, spring rings, a wooden comb, numerous Roman querns or handmills, the stone of some of which has been brought from quarries on the Rhine in Germany, and a huge battle-axe, are among the heterogeneous mass of antiquities thus singularly preserved.

The vast extent of the station, and of its numerous breast-works and ditches, forcibly impress a conviction of the prowess of the mighty people whose occupation of the country is thus perpetuated. Great indeed must be the want of susceptibility in the mind which can view ruins so stupendous without feelings of extreme

interest. The contemplative mind, surrounded with
such visible traces of so distant a period, will revert to
the past history of the sixteen centuries which have
since transpired, will mourn for the brave spirits who
here, as in nearly the whole world as then known,
erected their standard and left such gigantic memorials
of their triumphs,—will rejoice in the concurring events
which have converted the desolated field of war into a
peaceful and happy country,—and in the immediate as-
sociation of long-departed glories, with the solitary ruin
which now prevails, will find no ordinary lesson of the
fleeting and shadowy nature of earthly renown. Such
impressions are much strengthened by the familiar
nature of many of the fragments recently found. The
ruined station and heathen altars remind us of a warlike, superstitious, and powerful race of people, regard-
ed without any congenial feelings of sympathy. But
on examining such articles as shoes, combs, spoons,
and breast-pins,—their familiar and every-day nature
induces that social feeling which is always inspired by
similar usages or wants; and it is singularly interesting to contemplate them remaining in so perfect a state
after those who constructed and wore or used them
have slept the sleep of death for sixteen hundred
years.

A house formerly stood on the east side of the station, in which John Wallis, the historian of Northumberland, was born in 1714.

The present farm-house stands on the Maiden Way,
or Roman military way, which extends from Caervorran
on the Roman wall to Kirkby Thore in Westmoreland,
where it joins the great Roman road called Watling
Street. Its course may be plainly traced in the fields
south of the house, past the village of Whitley to
Gilderdale Burn, where it enters Cumberland. It may

be observed, that an old road from Brampton to Alston passed considerably nearer the station than the present one, and as only imperfect traces of it remain, it might possibly be mistaken for the Roman road. It passed on the west side of the station, crossed the Maiden Way near Whitley village, and had a bridge over Gilderdale Burn, only a few hundred yards below where the Maiden Way crosses. Thenceforth their courses southward are very different. The turnpike may be traced very plainly through a large pasture called Wanwood Bent, passing rather eastward and toward the town of Alston. The track of the Maiden Way is more obscurely seen winding obliquely and rather to the west up Gilderdale Forest: it continues between Park Fell and Scarberry, and may again be very distinctly seen for a considerable distance from the turnpike leading to Hartside, which crosses it within a few yards of the western boundary of the manor of Alston Moor. It is here about seven yards wide, and formed of large stones. After crossing Rowgill Cleugh, it ascends and passes over the highest ridge of the Penine Chain, about a mile north of the summit of Crossfell Mountain, continuing down the steep escarpment of that mountain to Milburn, and thence to Kirkby Thore.

On returning by the turnpike to Alston, Gilderdale Burn, at the distance of about half a mile from the station, divides the counties of Northumberland and Cumberland. On the 24th of July, 1829, these parts were visited by a dreadful storm of thunder and rain, which continued the whole of the afternoon and evening. The sides of the neighbouring mountains, notwithstanding their rapid declivity, were literally covered with sheets of water, which rolled down with resistless violence, in many places tearing up the surface, and in a great measure destroying the bridges over Gilderdale, Lort, and Thornhope Burns. The latter was entirely taken away, and the former had only the wall on one side left standing. Gilderdale Burn runs on a stratum of limestone, which, above Garrigill, forms the bed of the Tyne for upwards of four miles, and is hence called the Tyne bottom limestone. A little below the bridge, Gilderdale Burn sinks in this limestone, and pursues a subterraneous channel for some distance. About three quarters of a mile from this bridge, a footpath leads past a farm-house called Harbetlaw, and through fields to Tyne bridge at Alston; near which is a shot tower, which, with embrasures at the top and a house adjoining, has much the appearance of a church. It is 56 feet high, and is built over a shaft of nearly the same depth. The shot is brought out by a level at the base of the steep hill on which the tower is built.

CHAP. V.

CROSSFELL MOUNTAIN.

Ascent—Prospect—Sunrise—Western Descent—Dufton Pike, &c.

THE usual ascent of this gigantic mountain by strangers is from Garrigill Gate, between three and four miles from Alston. From this village an awkward road climbs in a very zigzag manner to the dark brow of a steep mountain fell called the Black-band Edge, which commands a fine view of the adjoining vale of Tyne. The road is continued in a nearly direct line over a flat and heathy moor, presenting a wild and sterile prospect, void of any remarkable feature save that of wide and solitary desolation. Even Crossfell does not seem greatly elevated, so much does its immense bulk and long flat summit destroy the effect of its altitude at a distance. But on a nearer approach, its huge and rugged sides assume a noble aspect, and when covered with snow a very sublime one. The admiration of this, however, as well as the unpleasing effect of so dreary a view, are alike counteracted by the care required in riding along a road of the most miserable description, the greater part of it being made entirely for the use of the mines, consists merely of rough stones loosely thrown on to prevent ore galloways sinking in the moss. The horses or ponies on which strangers usually ascend the greater part of the mountain, are left either at the Smelt Mill, four miles and a half from

Garrigill, or at Lang Kate Lock mining shop, which is a mile and a half further along the side of the mountain. By continuing three-quarters of a mile past this place, and then ascending the steep face of the mountain due south for the same distance, the highest summit is gained at a stone currock, erected by Col. Mudge when engaged with the trigonometrical surveys. The entire distance from Alston by this route is ten miles and a half.

To the tourist who is so fortunate as to be here in a clear atmosphere, a prospect is afforded which richly repays the laborious journey required to gain it. All the most prominent features of one of the most interesting portions of England are seen spread out in endless variety—hundreds of square miles of rich cultivated land, diversified with forests and innumerable and variously-coloured fields, lying like a map beneath the spectator, present a scene of unparalleled richness and beauty. No details, however minute, can convey an idea of the magnificent spectacle, and if the weather only prove favourable for the view, the tourist here runs no risk of being disappointed by overdone description, for no account, however florid, can equal, much less exceed, the attractions here presented to the delighted and astonished observer.

The following extracts are from notes of an excursion to Crossfell and the western declivities of the adjoining mountain ridge, by one of a party who spent a night on the summit of this mountain a few summers ago.

" We left Alston in the afternoon, and walked in an hour and a half to the summit of Rodderup Fell. The atmosphere was hazy, and the heat very oppressive. From this place Crossfell has a commanding appearance. We proceeded leisurely to the summit of this mountain, where we arrived at 7 o'clock, and found the rest of our party who had gone by Garrigill Gate. A hazy atmosphere still obscured the beautiful low countries west of the mountain. Soon after the sun's bright and fiery orb assumed a deep crimson colour, and sunk among dark and heavy clouds in the distant horizon.

" Alston Moor appeared perfectly clear, and presented a wide and sterile prospect ; its naked moors being fully exposed to view, and its cultivated portions too distant, and too much buried in the valleys, to impart a cheerful contrast to the dreary and extensive hills. Nothing remarkable appeared, save white volumes of mist, which slowly rose from the deep valleys at the base of the mountain.

" Having pitched a tent one hundred yards north of Col. Mudge's currock, we sat down at 9 o'clock to a very comfortable repast, and had the satisfaction of supping on one of the most elevated stations in the kingdom. Our coffee boiled with water fresh from the mountain spring, mixed with excellent cream, and drank with appetites heightened by mountain air and arduous exertion, had a truly delightful relish,—the more so as we had provided every comfort in abundance, and felt the highest gratification in accomplishing the journey. At 10 we were joined by some other friends, and spent an hour in rambling along the outskirts of the summit, in visiting Gentleman's Well, and surveying the stupendous masses of stone piled in tremendous confusion at the north extremity of the mountain, and which form the steep ascent or peak so observable from Alston. On some of these immense blocks we sat down, and viewed the western plains below, the luxuriant features of which were just discernible by the moonlight shining through a hazy atmosphere.

" The cold * was now as severe as the heat of the
preceding day had been oppressive, but for this we
had provided by sending on horseback extra suits of
clothes, which, with great coats, plaids, comforters, and
mittens, a good covering over the tent, a blazing fire
in front, and some excellent grog, sufficed to render
us very comfortable. An amusing tale, by the Ettrick
Shepherd, was read by one of the party till midnight,
when, putting out our lights, we lay down, but only
reposed, not slept. This was not owing to want of
comfort, but to the interest of the scene around us rendered impressively sublime by deep midnight silence,
and the moon's stately course through the clear canopy
above ; admiration of these dispelled all thoughts of
sleep. At one the morning began to dawn, and soon
shed its ' genial rays' along the distant horizon,
formed by the Cheviot, Rimside, and Simonside hills,
the deep purple hue of which, contrasted with the
golden sky behind, had a sublime effect. The thin
grey clouds floating in the clear blue sky above gradually assumed the most exquisite tints, until at 3
o'clock a long and thin dark cloud, which stretched
along the horizon, suddenly became a brilliant line of
refulgent light, a beautiful harbinger of the scarcely
more brilliant sun which soon after rose with inex-
pressible grandeur amid the silence and sublimity of
the vast scene before us. All nature seemed to re-
spond the deep and solemn feeling impressed by so
sublime a spectacle ; the ' wilderness and solitary place'
again became glad, and the desert seemed once more
to rejoice in the commencement of another day. With

* The Thermometer at Midnight was 42 degrees.
     At 1 in the Morning,   -   -   43 degrees.
     At 2 in the Morning,   -   -   41¾ degrees.
     At Sunrise, - - - - -   44 degrees.

such feelings we silently gazed on this glorious scene, until the solar beams illuminating the western portion of the island, we turned to contemplate its beauties as the lessening shade of the mountain presented them to our view.

"It is quite impossible to convey to those who have not witnessed it, a correct or even a tolerable idea of the view from Crossfell. So vast in extent—so rich in detail—so various in its features. The Cumbrian mountains piled in stupendous grandeur, range along the western horizon, and with Stanemoor and the mountains of Westmoreland on the south, and those of Scotland on the north, form a panorama of the most stupendous and magnificent scenery. The cultivated lands of Westmoreland and Cumberland have an exceedingly beautiful appearance, fraught with all the variety which can adorn the face of nature. Lakes and mountains, hills and valleys, fields and forests, towns and villages, heathy moors and flowery gardens, halls and cottages, the stately and the humble ' homes of England,' the ' tall ancestral trees' and the *deep* woody dells, the venerable cathedral and the village spire; these and innumerable other details are spread over the vast expanse so fully exposed to view from the summit of Crossfell mountain.

" A little after sunrise, the air being very cold and piercing, we struck our tent and formed with it a screen to the windward of a large stone flag, which we raised for a table, and placed stone seats around. After partaking of an excellent breakfast, we repaired to Gentleman's Well; here we washed and dressed, and after packing up our superfluous clothing, made by active exercise a gradual transition from the cold of a Crossfell night to the increasing warmth of a burning midsummer day. After examining the country through

glasses, assisted in the local topography of the districts
by maps of the neighbouring counties, we commenced
the descent of the western escarpment of the mountain.
This side is much steeper than the other, a prominent
and very prevailing feature in this chain of mountains,
and indeed of mountains generally. After a gradual
descent of about a mile, we arrived at the edge of a
very steep declivity of great depth, and nearly covered
with tremendous masses of broken rock and projecting
cliffs. At the bottom of this rolls the fierce and rumbling torrent of Crowdundle Beck, which here divides
the counties of Westmoreland and Cumberland. To
the left, the desolate ravine through which it flows
passes the mountain side, and, widening on the other
hand, forms a fearful but sublime amphitheatre of
great height and steepness. The descent of these rugged steeps by those unaccustomed to them can only be
effected by digging with the heels a support for each
succeeding step—holding by masses of stone or by the
short and slippery grass, or by climbing over the screeds
or immense masses of broken stone. On the opposite
side we encountered similar difficulties, stretching wide
paces from rock to rock, or among large loose blocks,—a
false step, an infirm grasp, or a yielding stone, might
have precipitated us to the bottom. After leaving this
ravine, we again proceeded on our descent to near the
base of the mountain, three miles from the summit.
Here we rested, and viewed with much admiration
the prospect of the mountain we had descended. Successive ranges of steep projecting hills form the fore-
ground. Beyond these rise the tremendous and precipitous cliffs of the north side of the ravine we had
passed—their surface beautifully varied by the visible
bassett of the strata—the pale hazel and the dark
mountain limestone ; and in the midst may be traced

the bold rising and solidity of the Great Rundle bed
or Melmerby scar limestone. Above these rose the
extreme summit of the mountain, at this time beautifully clear, and tinged with a delicate purple shade,
which, like a royal robe, invested the highest summit of the Penine Alps.

" Our route was now directed to Dufton Pike, a
steep and lofty hill distant apparently about two, but
in reality seven miles from the top of Crossfell, so very
deceiving is distance among these mountains, which,
by their immensity, confound all ideas of proportion.
Hill after hill, vale after vale, were passed, and at every
eminence we reached, our distance from Dufton Pike
seemed increased, instead of lessened; and when at
length one only moor extended between its base and
ius, it seemed as far distant, if not more so than it had
appeared, four hours before, from the commanding
summit of Crossfell.

" Our path lay along the western base of the Penine
Chain, and was crossed by numerous ravines. Down
the steep sides of these we ran or climbed as best
suited, and sometimes slid with great ease and velocity
when the ground would admit. At one place the
leader sat down on the edge of a steep brae, and slid
about 150 feet, followed by the rest of the party,
who in less than a minute looked with some surprise
at the eminence so swiftly and pleasantly descended.
The heat, now increased by the reflection of bare hills,
became very oppressive, and a partial bathe in the
rivulets which we crossed occasionally afforded an
agreeable refreshment.

" Arrived at the north part of Dufton Pike, a perfect hay-stack or pyramid of a mountain, we found
that the shortness and dryness of the burnt-up grass

F

rendered the ascent both difficult and dangerous, and, after proceeding some distance up, we abandoned the intention of gaining the summit, which the excessive warmth, with our previous fatigue, would have rendered an arduous undertaking. We therefore sat down, and dined where we were, and afterwards slid with great speed to the base.

"Crossfell commands an exceedingly fine view, so does Dufton Pike, and with this great advantage, that while the foreground of the one is formed by dreary fells, that of the other consists of the luxuriant tresses of fertility which embrace the very sides, not of a brown and dreary moor, but of a steep green hill rising suddenly from well-cultivated land. Far as the eye can reach, it beholds verdure smiling over an extensive and beautiful country—the soil is tinged with the ruddy colour of the prevailing stratum of red sandstone—the waters of the Eden and other streams sparkled like molten silver with the reflection of meridian rays, and flowed through a landscape of such inimitable loveliness as to seem a perfect paradise —while the huge and rugged but sublime formation of the distant Cumbrian mountains as forcibly bespoke the wreck of a disjointed world. Such was our prospect from this place, a prospect so rich and gay—so bright and fair in some respects, and so terribly sublime in others, that our enthusiastic admiration of its beauties was only equalled by the surprise that any portion of this earth should present so brilliant a spectacle."

An account of Crossfell Mountain, published in the Gentleman's Magazine for 1747, commences thus :— " A mountain that is generally *ten months buried in snow and eleven in clouds* cannot fail of exciting the attention and curiosity of a traveller." If these dread features then constituted its only claims to attention and curiosity, they are, however inviting, now entirely forfeited. Winter indeed slowly and reluctantly withdraws his hoary mantle from the bosom of this alpine hill, and mists and clouds delight to hover round its summit; but these form poor attractions for a stranger, and their comparative duration as stated above is greatly exaggerated. Indeed the writer himself humorously enough adds, " Being the 13th of August, *and a long drought and hot season,* we were not able to find the *least relics of snow* in places most likely for it, which is very extraordinary." The same writer describes the ascent of Crossfell from Blackburn as follows:—" We are now so much environed with large and extended morasses, rocks, and mountains, that they exhibit a very frightful appearance; not the vestige of a house, except some old *shiels,* where, in former ages, the people had resorted, like the Asiatic Tartars, to graze their cattle in summer—a practice now disused. There were a few sheep, but no deer that we could see, though there are several on the heights; and, notwithstanding the extraordinary drought, the water followed our horses' footsteps for miles together, except where the ground was rotten."

" We had now ascended gradually about three miles through very broken morassy wastes, when the mountain began to rise in three very formidable ascents, very steep, in the manner of Mount Lebanon, piled one above another, with large and extensive plains to each of them, and loose shivery stones on brows, very troublesome to the horses, which we were obliged sometimes to quit. This continued for two miles more, when we got on the edge of the highest, which forms a capacious plain of several hundred acres if you reckon from the east ascent, but of such barren soil that there was not so much as a single leaf of grass, herb, or plant to be found in so large a plain, exclusive of a few of those rings attributed to fairies, some of which are perfect circles of the *gramen glumis variis* in botany, ascribed by Linnæus, in his description of the Baltic isles, to a particular quality of its affecting the dirtiest soil, where no grass can thrive. This immense plain has no other verdure, therefore, but a venerable aspect from the moss or down, and this can hardly draw a subsistence to support itself, so inconceivably barren is this distinguished eminence."

The height of Crossfell is variously stated, and has probably not been ascertained with great exactness. Donald makes it 3390, Pennant 3839, and Col. Mudge only 2901 feet above the level of the sea. Its latitude is stated, in Hutchinson's History of Cumberland, to be 54° 42′ 05″ north; and in computing its height, the Rev. William Richardson, in an account of the mountain, says, "its elevation from Lazonby Bridge, near Kirkoswald, is 910 or 912 yards, and allowing 6 yards more for the height of the bridge over the river Eden, it will be about 918 yards, and if you allow 80 yards for the fall of the river Eden into Solway Frith, the hill will even then be scarcely 1000 above the level of the sea. Its distance from Kirkoswald is 11 miles and 1040 yards."

He adds, " The most delightful sight—the most noble spectacle I ever saw, was the sun rising when I was on the summit of Crossfell, on the 18th day of June. It is infinitely grander than a setting sun."

CHAP. VI.

HARTSIDE:

Prospect—Comparison of other Mountain Views—Helm
Wind, &c.

———

THOSE who have not time or inclination to undertake
the laborious excursion to Crossfell, may enjoy a considerable portion of the view which it commands from
where the turnpike road from Alston to Penrith crosses
the highest ridge of the same mountainous chain at
Hartside—distant about six miles from the former
town. The excellent state and very gradual ascent
of the road render this station easily accessible, though
the summit level is probably the highest turnpike in
England. Here a prospect of almost boundless extent,
comprising a large portion of the county of Cumberland, is presented to the view. The most varied and
luxuriant cultivation extends over immense plains and
gently undulated hills as far as the eye can distinguish
these lesser features of the landscape—chequered with
innumerable divisions, with waving forests and the
richest variety of corn lands, fertile meadows, and
bright green pastures intersected with fine hedge-
rows. The dark umbrage of village trees contrasted
by the lively aspect of the whitewashed houses, while
mountain streams, lakes, and rivers may be traced as
on a map. The features of the distant view are uncommonly grand; the mountains of the lake district

extend along the western horizon, presenting a spectacle of unequalled magnificence; the lake of Ulls-
water, at twenty miles distance, is clearly distinguished
in the midst of the romantic recesses, while the tower-
ing forms of Skiddaw and Saddleback, powerfully
impress the character of sublimity on this tremendous
and precipitous chain of mountains; in the north-west,
the city of Carlisle, and the fine scenery adjoining, are
plainly seen; behind them, the Solway Frith stretches
across the country, and beyond its smooth and silver
surface, rise the shores and distant hills of Scotland,
forming the horizon of this inimitable prospect, which
in favourable weather excites the unqualified astonishment and admiration of every beholder.   It may be
observed that the atmosphere is seldom so perfectly
clear as to afford a distinct view of this extensive scene
in every direction; but though a sight of the innumerable minute details which are then visible is extremely interesting, yet the general effect is often not so
fine as when some portions of it are partially obscured.
Clouds floating on the mountain summit—oceans of
dense mists floating over the immense plains below,
here and there pierced by little eminences which seem
like islands—and often by evaporating gradually,
unfold the beauties of the scene in a most sublime
manner.   The shades of evening add depth and
blueness to the mountainous horizon, and the reflection
of the setting sun in the Solway Frith, at such
times, seems like a broad line of fire drawn across the
country.   These are a few of the varieties which often
fully compensate for the want of an extremely clear
atmosphere.   The best station for commanding this
prospect is on a projecting brow of the hill at Toot-
hope, close to the edge of, and about half a mile along
the old road which branches to the left from the new

line beside a small shieling immediately on gaining the summit of the fell.

As a mountain view, the spread-out, map-like character of the country and great variety of prospect afforded by Hartside, are probably unequalled in these kingdoms. It is, however, difficult, if not presumptuous, to award such a distinction amidst the varied and magnificent scenes which nature in this favoured isle so often presents. Much admiration had this prospect ever afforded to the writer of these notices of it, but it was not until after witnessing other remarkable and far-famed prospects from other mountains that he was led to form so favourable an estimate of the comparative merits of the view from Hartside.

To many of these, indeed, a high degree of admiration must be awarded. The wide extended plains and gently undulated hills near Stirling, silvered with the tortuous windings of the Forth, and "gloomed" with the frowning barrier of the Ochils, and in the blue aërial distance the faintly-seen Ben Lomond and the chain of the Grampians, even in the dimness of this vast distance indicating by their rugged outline the terrible grandeur of their romantic solitudes. Arthur's Seat, looking proudly down on a city of palaces—combining at once the attractions of picturesque beauty and of architectural magnificence; on one side, the Montpelier of Scotland, its fine lake, smooth lawns, and shady trees, on another, the rocky scars of Salisbury crags— beyond them, a beautiful country scattered over with pleasant fields, and villages, and trees, and the tame flatness of part of the distant horizon varied by the bolder outline of the Pentlands. Eildon Hill, near Melrose, commands an almost perfect panoramic prospect of one of the fairest portions of Scotland, which, however grand and extensive as it is, has no horizon of sea or mighty mountain to complete the "sublime" of this species of landscape.   The rounded acclivities and want of varied profile in the eastern portion of the Cheviots, and the long and dark extended moors of Ettrick, form an interesting but certainly not a grand horizon.

The highest of the Cheviots commands an almost boundless extent of view.   If hills, like heads, have phrenological bumps, then on Cheviot may we look for a large developement of "extensiveness," for such constitutes the principal feature of the view which it affords.   Mere extent, however, is more calculated to employ the judgment, or please the imagination, than to delight the eye.   The most picturesque objects or finely cultivated land, when far removed, are too minute and indistinguishable to afford much beauty. From Cheviot, the cultivated portions of the view are very distant, and the intervening space is filled with a dreary range of dark and flat moors and hills,—bare, without the redeeming ruggedness of diluvial wreck to impart a stubborn grandeur or suddenness of elevation, to create that picturesque variety which so beautifully characterizes the western portion of the Cheviot range.

Such is a rapid sketch of the general features of some deservedly admired prospects, but a high degree of admiration of them has served only to confirm an unqualified preference to the views afforded by the Penine range of hills—combining, as they do, an almost boundless extent, luxuriant cultivation,—a sublime amphitheatre of stupendous mountains—the placid lake in the bosom of their deep recesses, and the lofty hills of Scotland rising beyond the broad and silvery sea. Whether such a prospect deserves the eminent distinction of being the finest in all England, must be left to

abler judges and more experienced eyes to determine.
It is, however, probably beyond all doubt, that no view
in these kingdoms, any way comparable to it, is of so
easy access, the summit of Hartside being crossed by
an excellent turnpike, which, though it leaves the best
station somewhat to the south, yet presents a considerable extent of the amazing view thus imperfectly at-
tempted to be described.

The mere sight of such extensive prospects, however interesting, is the least delightful part of the pleasure they afford. Deep and solemn veneration of the
Great Framer of so beautiful a world, either is, or
ought to be, impressed on every one who is permitted
to enjoy such evidences of the goodness and power of
the Author of nature. Every portion of the ample
page there spread before the astonished eye utters one
voice of silent but impressive praise, and cold and dark
must be the chambers of his heart who responds not
to it,—who rejoices not in the richness and beauty of
the fertile plains, admires not the august image of
Deity impressed in the glory of His works, and rises
not from the contemplation of them, to the beneficent
Being whose presiding care sustains them all!—who
not only adorned the earth with beauty, and enriched
it with fruitfulness, but even in the barren hills poured
hidden treasures of wealth for the service of His crea-
tures.

Sentiments thus vividly impressed by the contemplation of such scenes, have an ennobling tendency,
and afford the most agreeable subjects of future medi-
tation. It has been very beautifully observed, that
" book learning is perhaps the least part of the education of the species. Nature is the mightiest and kindli-
est of teachers. The rocks and unchanging hills give
to the mind a sensation of existence beyond that of the

perishable body.   The flowing stream images to the
soul an everlasting continuity of tranquil enjoyment.
The brave o'erhanging firmament imparts, even to the
most rugged swain, some consciousness of the universal
brotherhood of those over whom it hangs.   The affec-
tions ask not leave of the understanding to glow, and
spread, and kindle, to shoot through all the frame a
tremulous joy, or animate to holiest constancy.   We
taste the dearest blessedness of earth without being
able to express it in mortal language.   The purest
delights grow tenderly beneath our feet, all who will
stoop may gather them, and, gifted with divine imagination, may walk in glory and in joy upon the mountain side."

The *helm wind* is a curious local phenomenon, which
occurs along several miles of the western side of these
mountains, and to the violence of which the traveller
will be occasionally exposed.   It derives its name from
being accompanied by a long band or cloud stretching
like a helmet over the summit of the hills, and occurs
more frequently in the spring and autumn than at other
times.   Its duration is very various, from a few hours
to a few days.

The following interesting notices of this singular
phenomenon are chiefly extracted from Hutchinson's
History of Cumberland.

" Upon the summits of this lofty ridge of mountains there frequently hangs a vast column of clouds,
in a sullen and drowsy state, having little movement;
this heavy collection of vapours frequently extends
several miles in length, and dips itself from the
summit, half way down to the base of these eminences; and frequently, at the same time, the other
mountains in view are clear of mist, and shew no
signs of rain.   This *helm* or cloud, exhibits an aw-

ful and solemn appearance, tinged with white by the sun's rays that strike the upper parts, and spreading a gloom below, over the inferior parts of the mountains, like the shadows of night. When this collection of vapour first begins to gather upon the hills, there is to be observed, hanging upon it, a black strip of cloud, continually flying off and fed from the white part, which is the real *helm;* this strip is called the *helm bar,* as, during its appearance, the winds are thought to be resisted by it, for, on its dispersion, they rage vehemently upon the valleys beneath. The direction of the *helm bar* is parallel to that part of the main cloud or collection of vapour that is tinged with white by being struck with the sun's rays, the *bar* appears in continual agitation, as boiling or struggling with contrary blasts ; while the *helm* all this time keeps a motionless station. When the *bar* is dispersed, the winds that issue from the helm are sometimes extremely violent ; but that force seems to be in proportion to the real current of the winds which blow at a distance from the mountains, and which are frequently in a contrary direction, and then the *helm wind* does not extend above two or three miles ; without these impediments it seldom sweeps over a larger tract than twelve miles, perhaps from the mere resistance of the lower atmosphere. It is remarkable, that at the base of the mountain the blasts are much less violent than in the middle region ; and yet the hurricane is sometimes impetuous even there, bearing every thing before it, when, at the distance of a few miles, there is a dead calm, and a sunny sky. The spring is most favourable to this phenomenon. The *helm wind* will sometimes blow for a fortnight, till the air in the lower regions, warmed before by the influence of the sun, is thereby rendered piercing cold.

Mr. Ritson thus speaks of the *helm wind* :—" the *helm wind* is generated in that enormous cloud, which, like a *helmet*, covers the summit of Crossfell. It is there particularly favoured by circumstances; for on one side there is a plain of about thirty miles in breadth, in some places; and on the other no hills to rival that from whence it comes. This wind is not much taken notice of in natural history: yet the Dutch, by the iron chains with which they are obliged to moor their ships at the Cape of Good Hope, bear ample testimony to the fury of such a one. It has been met with by the late voyagers in the south seas; it is said to have been felt in the straits of Gibraltar; and I have no doubt but mariners and travellers have found it in many other places, though they may not have observed it with care, or may have given it other names."

Mr. Richardson remarks, "that in the vicinity of these mountains the air is generally very clear and healthy, owing perhaps to the violent *helm wind* in the months of December, January, February, March, and April; but the inhabitants of the counties immediately influenced by that wind are more subject to rheumatic complaints than those at a greater distance. The summit of Crossfell and the regions a little lower are sometimes clear, when the vale is covered with a fog; I have been upon the mountain when that has happened, and the spectacle is curious, as the clouds appear firm, though uneven, like a boisterous, disturbed ocean, all distant sounds are at that time heard distinctly, and strike the ear in a very singular manner, as they seem to issue under your feet. As to the *helm*, the cloud does not always rest upon the top of the hills, but is sometimes several degrees higher, and does

not always preserve a regular form; neither is there
always a *helm bar*, for that phenomenon only appears
when the wind at a little distance blows from the west.
I have sometimes observed four or five of these *helm
bars* within five miles of the hills, and then the wind
blew irregularly, sometimes from the east and sometimes from the west. It appears to me to be the same
kind of phenomenon as that at the Cape of Good
Hope, described by Sparman. When the snow appears
upon the hills the winds then blow with great violence. Swinburne, I think, mentions something similar in Sicily, and Volney at Alexandria. May it not
be accounted for by the air being considerably colder
on the summit of these hills, than in the country
whither it rushes with so much violence? I have
found by a thermometer, that it is 14° colder on the
top of Crossfell than at the bottom, indeed I did but
prove that once, but three or four times I found it 12°
and frequently 10°. The name of *helm* seems to be
derived from the Saxon, and implies, in our language,
a *covering*. Its appearances, according to my remarks,
have been that of a white cloud resting upon the
summits of the hills, extending even from Brough to
Brampton; it wears a bold, broad front, not unlike a
vast float of ice standing on edge; on its first appearance, there issues from it a prodigious noise, which, in
grandeur and awfulness, exceeds the roaring of the
ocean. Sometimes there is a *helm bar*, which consists
of a white cloud ranged opposite to the *helm*, and holds
a station various in its distances, sometimes not more
than half a mile from the mountain, at others, three or
four miles: sometimes it is in breadth a quarter of a
mile, at others a mile at least; this cloud prevents the
wind blowing further westward. The sky is generally
visible between the helm and the bar, and frequently

G

loose bodies of vapours or small specks of clouds are
separated from the helm and the bar, and flying across
in contrary directions, both east and west, are seen to
sweep along the sky with amazing velocity.   When
you arrive at the other side of the *bar cloud*, the wind
blows eastward, but underneath is a dead calm, or
gusts of wind from all quarters.   The violence of the
wind is generally greatest when the helm is highest
above the mountains.   The cold air rushes down the
hill with amazing strength, so as to make it very difficult for a person to walk against it.   I have frequently
been under the necessity of turning my back to take
breath at every ten yards at least ; it mostly comes in
gusts, though it sometimes blows with unabated fury
for twenty-four hours ; and continues blowing at intervals for three, four, five, and even six weeks.   I have at
different times walked into the cloud, and found the
wind increase in violence, till I reached the mist floating on the side of the hill ; when once entered into
that mist I experienced a dead calm.   If the *helm* is
stationed above the mountain, and does not rest upon
it, it blows with considerable violence immediately
under the helm.   I once walked so far on the Alston
Moor side, till the wind blew from the mountain ;
hence I supposed that the wind rushes down on each
side, and shepherds have frequently told me they
have observed it to be so."

   To these interesting notices of so very remarkable
a phenomenon, it may be added, that the appearance
of the helm bar may be considered as chiefly appear-
ing only to those on the western side of the mountain.   At such times, Crossfell, as seen from Alston
Moor, does not present any of the remarkable
features so fully described in the preceding accounts,
with the exception of what is a very common cha-

racteristic, a covering of dark and heavy mists. It has been thought by some that the violent gusts of the helm wind flow in separate streams as it were through the atmosphere. In riding on horseback or in a gig along the western base of the Penine Chain, the air has been found almost perfectly calm eight or ten feet from the ground, while at the same time the tops of the neighbouring trees have been violently bent to and fro with the force of a very powerful wind.

Charles Slee, Esq., in a paper on this subject, read before the Royal Physical Society, in January, 1830, observes, " I have no theory to offer by way of explaining the *helm*, inasmuch as some of the facts relative to it, appear to me hardly compatible with the laws of matter and motion. Such, for instance, as the perfect repose of the bar when the current is strongest. Such also is the very circumscribed limits within which it exerts its action. It does not appear to have any dependance on the presence of the sun, for it happens during the night as well as during the day. The circumstance of the helm only occurring when the wind is easterly has led me sometimes to conjecture that an accumulation of air takes place on the eastern side of the mountain, which after a time overcomes the weight of the superincumbent atmosphere, and forces itself over the summit and down the opposite side."

These and other circumstances attending it require further investigation before much can be said with correctness as to the cause of so remarkable a phenomenon.

CHAP. VII.

ALE BURN CAVERN—HUDGILL BURN CAVERN.

IT has already been observed that the great limestone
is the thickest and nearly the highest calcareous stratum that occurs in these mining districts, and that its
bassett or outcrop forms in many places the limit of
cultivated land and of human habitations. These characteristics may be readily observed in the steep hills
on the north side of Ale Burn, which, rising on the
verge of Whitfield Fell, falls by a steep and rocky
channel into the river Tyne near Randalholme, and
forms part of the southern boundary of the county of
Northumberland. A walk of about two miles from
Alston to some parts of this burn, presents to the

geologist a good opportunity of examining this stratum; and the less scientific tourist may probably find
some interest in the rocky scenery and singular caverns
which here occur. The principal of these is situated
in the great limestone; and the entrance to it is by a
level from the north side of Ale Burn, a few yards
above where it is crossed by a bridge near Clargill.
This level is drawn in a direction nearly north and
south; at the distance of about fifty fathoms is a small
opening at the roof communicating with what in mining phraseology is called a *rise*, and which, awkward
and inconvenient as it is, is the only mode yet discovered of gaining access to the cavern. The following notes descriptive of this singular place were made
during a subterraneous survey of its dark and gloomy
chambers.

" After climbing from the level roof by an opening
barely sufficient to admit our passage, we ascended a
rise of about 30 feet in height, by means of sticks or
stemples placed alternately at two opposite sides of the
rise. On gaining the top, we entered with some
difficulty into a small circular opening in the limestone,
just large enough to permit our creeping along it on
hands and knees. On proceeding a few fathoms in
this uncomfortable posture, the noise of rushing waters
was heard increasing until it became very loud, and
we soon found ourselves near the summit of a spacious
vault or natural cavern 23 feet high, 13 feet wide, and
16 feet long. We climbed down the nearly perpendicular side to a stream of water which passes the
whole length of the cavern, and at this time containing
as much water as Ale Burn. This rivulet seems partly
fed by the springs of Ale Burn, and in rains is much
increased by the surface water poured into it by means of

3

numerous swallow holes. Having descended, we turned past a projecting screen of rock, and from thence gained access to the continuation of the cavern westward. Here the natural curiosities which present themselves, if they deserve not the very lavish expressions of surprise and admiration often bestowed on similar scenes, at least deserve this, that they well repay the difficulty experienced in visiting them, and which to persons unaccustomed to mining excursions is by no means inconsiderable. It must be kept in mind that it is merely a limestone cavern, which, though exceedingly curious as such, is not possessed of the varied and splendid attractions of some celebrated caverns. Its dimensions vary considerably, being in some places from 20 to 30 feet high, and in others it is nearly filled with large loose blocks of limestone, the passage through the interstices of which is both awkward and dangerous. The sides present a curiously-fretted surface, moulded by the long-continued action of water into a variety of singular forms, some of which are truly remarkable. It is interesting to observe the process of this slow but constant operation, for the water gradually wearing the channel by which it first enters the cavern, falls successively on different portions of the rock below, until, in the course of years, the whole of the side of the cavern have been subjected to this fantastic chisel of nature. Many of these grotesque forms, especially when dimly seen, need little aid from the imagination to represent the images of various animals and other objects. In one place we observed an almost exact profile of the human face. The idea of the head and neck of foxes and eagles was often suggested by projecting pieces of rock; and in a small cavern, branching from the main one, four or five singularly-shaped pieces of limestone

seemed like a consultation of various animals suddenly
changed to stone.

" After proceeding upwards of a hundred yards
along the cavern, we saw a vein of lead ore which
crosses it, and from which some of our party worked
a few specimens of *galena*. From this place westward
the cavern becomes much straiter, so that in some
places where the roof had fallen, we could only proceed by lying on our breasts, and getting forward
through the narrow chasm as well as we could. At
length the stream of water entered a very low and narrow passage, into which we waded on our hands and
knees until nearly all our lights being lost, we were
compelled to return. Chaff put into the water here is
said to have come out at the surface at Barhagh about
three miles distant.

" On returning to where we first entered the cavern,
we proceeded along the first chamber, and by a low
passage entered a second 26 feet wide, of very irregular
width, but at breast height about 26 feet in one direction. At the east end of this is a double entrance to a
third cavern 30 feet long, 22 feet high, and 13 feet
wide. This entrance is divided by a curious natural
pillar (represented in the annexed wood cut) about
13 feet high, and measuring at the base not quite
4½ feet in circumference. This slender support appears to be shrinking, and will probably soon yield
to the immense weight of the massive rock which
it supports. A waterfall at the west end of this cavern
presents a fine spectacle. The water falls over a ledge
of rock in an equal stream 9 feet wide and 5½ feet
high. Above it huge blocks of limestone are tumbled in magnificent ruin, which, with the reverberated
noise of the falling stream, excite sensations in which
terror and sublimity are strongly blended."

The bassett of the great limestone for about a quarter of a mile above the level mouth exhibits numerous
indications of the cavern, the course of which indeed
is discernible at some distance by the numerous swallow holes along it.   Some of these open into small
caverns, doubtless communicating with the principal
one ; and to those who have not an opportunity or want
the courage to view the interior, some of these lesser
caverns may afford a faint idea of its nature.   In them
also the water may be seen silently modeling their
fretted sides, but the few specimens in them are very
inferior to those in the main cavern.   Exactly opposite
the old road to Allendale is one of these smaller caverns
near a sheep-wash in Ale Burn, where the rude face
of limestone scars, the blocks which impede the
rapid stream, and the falls of the latter in its steep
descent, form some interesting scenery.   The sides of
this cavernous grotto abound with various mosses and
brachia ; in one corner is an opening which appears to
communicate with the main cavern, and by which it is
probable that an easy access might be had into it.

The level by which the present entrance was
discovered, was driven by the London Lead Company about fifty years ago, when one of the workmen
named Rumney lost his life by a massive piece of rock
falling on him. A party who subsequently explored
the cavern were placed in imminent danger by the loss
of their lights.

In the celebrated lead mine of Hudgill Burn is
another but less curious and picturesque cavern in the
great limestone. It was discovered in the spring of
1816 by a rise of six fathoms high from the level, 391
fathoms from the entrance of the mine. This rise was in
a vein (supposed to be Hudgill Burn third sun vein) at
this place not exceeding 4 inches in width.   The

cavern was found to be terminated to the north by this vein, which at the extremity presented a crust of the burnt-like matrix or *rider* common in veins, and contained a thin rib of *galena* rich in silver. This vein improved to the eastward so much, that, at 30 fathoms from the shake or cavern, it was worked at seven shillings a bing, and continued rich until cut off by the thick alluvial deposit of the side of the mountain. On the west side of the cavern the same vein in 10 fathoms dwindled to nothing. It is stated by some of the miners that no veins have been discovered to come through the cavern, and that no traces of veins are to be seen in it as at Ale Burn.

The following notes, descriptive of this cavern, are extracted from the Newcastle Magazine, Sept. 1820. They are attributed to a military gentleman, who explored it with a party in Feb. 1818.

" At about 4 P. M. being dressed in the working habiliments of the miners, and seated in ore waggons, two in each, *vis a vis,* we were hurled along into the interior region of the mountain of Middle Fell.

" A lighted candle folded round with clay to prevent its melting by the heat of the hand, was carried by each person, and the ponies trudged in steady pace along the adit or level, with each its own candle suspended at the collar, beneath the breast. In this order the whole proceeded in silence, gazing upon the different strata that appeared in the roof and sides of the level for perhaps nearly half a mile. When we arrived at a part where another adit branches off to a different working in the mine, the boys conducting the horses then stopped, and the party got out to walk on foot along the right-hand level, with each his own light. In this passage there is a running stream of water drawn off from the mine, and the working parts are dry.   We passed air pipes, rising sumps or shafts, and some large masses of rich ore, piled up in open spaces on the side of the level, ready to be conveyed out to the bank.

" The party advanced, viewing with much curiosity and pleasure the signs of persevering energy and art which the mining works presented.

" Pursuing the subterraneous route by direction of two of the owners of this rich mine, for a distance we supposed to be nearly a quarter of a mile farther, our attention was arrested by a clattering noise a little way in front, occasioned, as we soon understood, by the stones and rubbish, from working, falling down a shaft upon cross-sticks, fixed alternately, a long step, one above each other at right angles, serving as a ladder, by which the workmen ascended to a vein above this shaft which opened into the cavern.   Up this shaft we had to scramble near 30 feet from one cross rafter to another, by hands and feet; an exertion of some diffi-culty, for these cross sticks were in places so far distant as to require all the active agility of youth to mount them, and some of our party were somewhat wearied by the progress they had already made.   Having ac-complished this our most arduous task, the entrance into the cavern or chasm was perceived.   During our clambering up to this part the working ceased, and the men offered their hands and assistance with be-coming and manly civility.   They then conducted us into the cavern, at the entrance of which they were pursuing their trial of a vein of no great promise.   The wonderful art attained in splitting the hard limestone rock by blasting, &c., to unfold the stores of nature, and to realize her treasures, strikes the senses of those unaccustomed to such work with astonishment.

" We entered the cavern—a light was sent forward, which showed the direction to be in a straight line for a great distance. The light appeared dim, and like a star peeping through a dingy cloud. The width varies from about three to six feet, as I thought, but we did not then measure either the width or the height. The roof has along its centre an indentation the whole length, and the chasm appeared somewhat wider at the top than it is at the bottom ; which, with the groove or rent in the middle of the roof, impressed a conception on the mind, of the sides having been thrown to recline backwards by some convulsion of nature. The groove is shallow, and appears like a wound healed up, leaving the scar as a mark of the injury formerly received.

" Advancing about half way, we came to a thin rock which divided our passage into two. We pursued the right-hand passage, now become so narrow, that a bulky man could scarcely get through, but it widened a little farther on. As we passed along, several openings and small recesses on our right and left were seen, but not of a sort to exite much interest, until we reached the far end of this passage, where there is an open space equal to a room of ordinary size, with a beautiful cabin on one side, nearly square, lined with smooth jet-black walls, richly spangled with stalactites, that sparkle equal to brilliants of the first water. The solemn grandeur of this place inclined the whole to pause, and contemplate the sublimity of the novel scene around us. We rested on the floor of solid limestone, and gazed on this charm of nature with awe and wonder. When I beheld a scene so superior to what can be produced by all the arts of man on earth, I could not conceal my regret that such

treasures should be made so difficult of access, that
they should be where—

> " At each step
> " Solemn and slow the shadows darker fall,
> " And all is awful, list'ning gloom around."

" The substance of so jet a black with which this
charming little cabin is lined, is called by miners
'black jack.'   It contains a portion of the ore of
zinc, and is smelted for its valuable produce, in great
demand throughout this realm for potteries, medical
purposes, brass, &c.   In this beautiful little room,
there are two openings, in form nearly square, from
the floor upwards, about $1\frac{1}{2}$ foot each side, lined with
substance the same, and embellished with glittering
spar, of exquisite brilliancy.   These transparent particles are very regularly distributed over the walls,
neither too thick nor too thin, to give the effect of
genuine taste and finish: but the process of nature is
going on, and that brilliant spar will most probably
become a thick crust, if not impeded by the hand of
the workman, and will in time attain to a solid mass
of quartz, of which numerous large pieces are found
in these mines.

" While we rested here, men were sent farther in advance, to explore the extent and nature of the several
low and narrow passages and openings in the rock,
which communicated with this open space; and having
taken hold of the end of a clew of pack-thread, to direct
their retrograde steps by the same way, they tried to
advance:—they proceeded on hands and knees, or feet,
as necessity dictated, a considerable way forward in
the largest openings they could find, until they were
called back by the voice and a tug of the line.   They
found no end to these numerous intersecting openings in the rock, the passages of which are extremely

intricate and dangerous, without proper precautions taken; for, to retrace exploring steps in such a labyrinth, if lights should fail, without a clew or their companions stationed as we were in the main track, would be to hazard their lives.

" Our curiosity on that occasion being gratified, we commenced on our return, by the same passage before described, but discovered some other passages which communicated with it, and in which some of our fellow travellers ventured to wander, and were able to join us again, without being obliged to return to the part where they entered the by-way.

" The length of the main chasm is 320 yards. Evident signs would seem to prove that this cavern and all its communicating fissures have been filled, at no very distant period, with water, and the probability is, it has been drained off by the adits in the mine, in which there runs, as I said before, a constant stream from some contiguous part of the works. The rocks of the cavern are covered by a sooty mucus in nearly a dried state, which, it may be presumed, was generated by the stagnant water and impure air, previous to its draining. There is a little mud left on the bottom of the cavern in a moist state, and the smell tends to confirm the conjecture of these concavities having been a reservoir for thousands of years, and drained off by the level of the mine. It appeared to me that some little ventilation passes through the whole, which might have been so ever since the water was let off; for the air from the level would follow the vent of the stream, and since the opening to the cavern was effected, a slight circulation of air would probably be created.

" There were, I think, nine of us altogether; we were in the cavern upwards of half an hour, and we

felt no material difficulty in breathing, while our candles, one to each, burnt sufficiently clear; which, with
the animal breathing, must together have consumed a
considerable quantity of pure air, such as to have
made a scarcity perceptible, if no fresh air had been
supplied."

This graphic description supersedes the necessity
of the author saying more than that his own inspection of this remarkable cavern enables him to state
that its details are as correct as they are highly interesting.

Near Gilderdale Burn, and about three miles from
Alston, is a limestone cavern which some accounts say
has been explored for above a mile. This, however,
is very apocryphal; and, admitting that it has been
entered for any considerable extent, yet distance,
unless actually measured, is extremely deceptive in
such precarious journeys. Other caverns of a similar
nature are to be found in various parts of the mining
districts; the preceding descriptions will, however,
convey a sufficiently correct idea of these features
of the mountain limestone. The pencil of the artist
has not been much employed on the romantic scenery
of these districts, but the mountain streams and waterfalls, and the interior of some of the limestone caverns
and mines, furnish abundant and highly interesting
pictorial subjects, which, now that the country is of
so easy and pleasant access, will, it is hoped, ere long,
be pourtrayed by some of our local artists.

Having, in this and the preceding chapter, noticed
such objects as are of common interest, and to be found
more or less in other parts of the kingdom, we come
now to describe the local peculiarities of Alston and its
vicinity. The Roman antiquities, mountain views, and
remarkable caverns, which are here to be found, inter-

esting as they certainly are, are yet of secondary importance to the geological features and mining interests of the country. Towards these, the investigations of science and the active speculations of commerce have long been directed, and the mines of Alston Moor are, with a large class of society in the north of England, the objects of more than ordinary interest.

The following notices of geology and mining are intended to afford occasional visitors such information as may enable them to understand what they see, without entering into minute scientific or practical details. Other readers, who have not had opportunities of viewing the mining districts, may perhaps by these brief descriptions be enabled to form a tolerably correct idea of the nature of the country—the formation of its hills—the phenomena of its veins and mineral treasures,—and of such other objects as constitute the more remarkable features of Alston and its adjoining dales.

CHAP. VIII.

GEOLOGY.

Comparative magnitude of the Earth, and its Strata. — Brief notice of Geological Theories. — Importance and interest of the Science. — Primary and Secondary Formations, &c.

GEOLOGY signifies a *discourse* or *reasoning* respecting the earth. Surely a more modest and appropriate term for the science it designates than that of Geognosy, or *knowledge* of the earth, which Werner and some other writers have adopted. For supposing the semi-diameter of the earth to be nearly four thousand miles, the *greatest possible extent* of human *knowledge* is included in a vertical distance of five miles, and this includes the highest mountains as well as the deepest mines. If, therefore, with a common scale and compasses, we draw part of a circle of eight inches radius, and make the circumference one hundredth part of an inch in thickness, a tolerably correct estimate may be formed of the exceedingly small portion of the earth of which we can possibly *know* any thing. It is most essential, in considering Geology, carefully to remember this very small proportion, as well as that which the human race bears to this apparently large, but really insignificant portion of the globe. Many things, which to our limited view seem so stupendous that we cannot comprehend any agency powerful enough to effect them, will, on proper consideration, be found very different from what we at first conceived. Thus, for instance, a stratum of limestone, 50 feet in thickness, being intersected by a vein, may be on one side raised (or, in mining phraseology, *thrown*) the height of its whole thickness, so that the bottom of the stratum on one side of the vein coincides with the top at the other. The view of so apparently great a disruption will give a very exaggerated idea of the agency which caused it, to what will be derived from a consideration of the subject on an extensive scale.

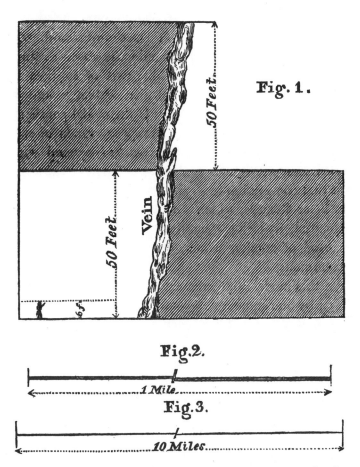

Fig. 1.

50 Feet

50 Feet

Vein

6 f.

Fig. 2.

1 Mile.

Fig. 3.

10 Miles.

The annexed diagram represents a person viewing such a phenomenon; and it may readily be supposed that a precipice of one hundred feet in height,

with its strata so much deranged, would, to so dimi-
nutive a being, seem a very stupendous object.
But in Fig. 2, where the stratum is represented
for a mile in length, the disruption appears far less
formidable.   And when, as in Fig. 3, a length of ten
miles with the thickness of 50 feet in proportion, is represented, it not only loses all appearance of vastness,
but seems absolutely trifling in comparison with its
extent.   Hence it will be readily comprehended that
if a model of a county, say of Northumberland, was
made on a scale of an inch to a mile, the above stratum
would be less than a hundredth part of an inch in
thickness, and a disruption of that extent would of
course be scarcely perceptible.   If the model consisted
of exceedingly thin laminæ of different kinds of clay
and stone, and was for a few minutes covered with
water, and afterwards suffered to dry, it is obvious
that that contraction in drying would produce various
cracks or fissures, which would become more or less
disjointed, and thus very simply produce a miniature
fac simile of results, which, on a larger scale, appear
so enormous.

On this model, be it remembered, the space represented by one square inch would contain all the people
of England; and if animalculæ were existing on the
model, and capable of thinking, they would be as
much staggered at these little, and, to the human eye,
almost imperceptible cracks, as we are at the cracks of
the great globe itself.   What amusement would we
derive by knowing the various schemes of these ani-
malculian philosophers to account for the mighty
changes which the model they lived on had undergone
—whereas a little water for a deluge—a few gentle
knocks for earthquakes,—and the application of fire
for subterranean heat,—would dissolve, and distort,

and vitrify as much as any geologist, whether Huttonian or Wernerian, could desire.

Without entering, therefore, into minute details, it
yet seems desirable to annex some account of the
general features and divisions of geological science to
these notices of the mining districts—not for the information of the scientific reader, but to give some general
ideas to those unacquainted with geology, which may
enable them better to understand the nature of mining
operations.

That the knowledge of geology was extremely
imperfect in the seventeenth century, may have been
already inferred from Sir John Pettus' singular theory
of the formation of hills and valleys. Scarcely less
ridiculous are many of the fancies which, in later
periods and with equal gravity, have been advanced
as profound speculations on this infant science.
During the progress of the last century, however, a
new light dawned on this hitherto mysterious subject,
and philosophical inquiry, while it dispelled the chi-
meras of former visionaries, was directed to the only
means by which any science can be successfully cultivated. The investigation of facts already known,
and patient and laborious research into the great
volume of nature, led to the discovery of many
curious and important phenomena in the construction
of the rocks and strata which constitute the outward
covering of the globe. At length the celebrated
Werner first laid a solid foundation for geology as a
science. By comparing the local rocks and strata
which he had observed with the geological structure
of foreign countries, he finally succeeded in arranging
the different strata of the earth into separate divisions
or formations. Some approach was thus made to
systematic order, accompanied by much theoretical

speculation, in which the various phenomena of
geology were chiefly referred to an *aqueous* origin.
Another theory was advanced by Dr. Hutton and
his followers, who chiefly differed from Werner, in
maintaining *fire* to be the great secondary cause in
the formation of the shell of the earth. Hence the
two opposing doctrines, which, under the names of
Wernerian and Huttonian theories, have caused so
much controversy.   Other writers have taken the
literal Mosaic account as the foundation of their
opinions, considering other theories as opposed to the
authority of the Scriptures. It is well known how
much a similar regard for the literal acceptation of
descriptive passages of Holy Writ not only impeded,
but violently opposed, the progress of astronomy. In
geology, as in astronomy, it is now generally admitted
that the details of the sacred Volume were written
for and addressed to the common understanding of
mankind, and not to solve the intricate perplexities
of science. How few cottagers understand the simple astronomical facts, that the sun is stationary, and
that the revolution of the earth alone causes its
apparent motion ! But who, either in the abodes
of the humble, or the schools of philosophy, can
fail to admire the sublime simile of the sun's
coming forth as a bridegroom, and *rejoicing as a
giant to run his course ?*   The book of Genesis, in
brief but magnificent poetry, informs us, that " *in
the beginning God created the heaven and the earth.*"
Whether the *Beginning* here spoken of was the same
period as the creation of mankind, or antecedent by
many ages, there is no means of deciding; though,
from many considerations, the latter is the more
probable conjecture. After all that has been devised
to account for the formation and successive changes

of the strata which compose the outer portion of the globe, the subject yet remains involved in many difficulties; and of all, even the most ingenious theories, it may too truly be said that "shadows, clouds, and darkness rest upon them."

But if we smile at the humorous fancies of some, or turn with doubt and dissatisfaction from the imperfect theories of others, let us not, therefore, consider the subject unworthy of attention or beyond the attainment of human intellect. On the contrary, much real importance must be attached to this study by every one who considers how much the well-being both of individuals and of nations depends on the improvement of every means, whether of knowledge or power, committed to our trust. In this country, where so much depends on the mineral products of the earth, too much attention cannot be given to a science so immediately connected with interests so important; and it is gratifying to perceive how rapidly a taste for this and similar departments of science has lately increased.

The institution of a Natural-History Society in Newcastle has already been the means of collecting many valuable additions to our local stores of geological knowledge; and it may be confidently hoped that, by its instrumentality, a series of facts will be collected, which may lead to the most valuable results.

Even a casual observer cannot fail to perceive that both fire and water have had, at some former period, a powerful agency, of which almost every rock and every vein bears testimony; but as to the precise period or operation of geological changes, mere theoretical discussions can lead to little or no practical use. Instead, therefore, of idle disputes on Neptunian and Plutonist dreams, let future researches be confined to the collection of carefully-observed facts. When these have been accumulated by industry and greatly increased by time, some Newton in geology may discover important and general laws guiding the successive changes of the strata. In the mean time we may rest assured that records of a patient and constant attention to actually existing phenomena are the most valuable additions which, at this period, can be made to the science of geology.

The general arrangement of what are called " formations" of the various rocks and strata which constitute the outward covering of the globe, is clearly exhibited in the following table, taken from the introduction to Conybeare and Phillips' Geology. It conveys not only a comprehensive view of the general character of each formation, but also a comparison of the arrangement of Werner and of other writers.

Character.	Proposed Names.	Wernerian Names.	Other Writers.
1. Formations chiefly of sand and clay.	Superior Order.	Newest Flœtz Class.	Tertiary Class.
2. Chalk.—Sand and clay.-----Calcareous freestones (oolites) & argillaceous beds. New red sandstone. Conglomerate and magnesian limesto.	Supermedial Order.	Flœtz Class.	Secondary Class.
3. Carboniferous rocks, comprising coal measures.— Carboniferous limestone.——Old red sandstone.	Medial Order.	Sometimes referred to the preceding and sometimes to the following class. Very often the coal measures are referred to the former, the subjacent limestone and sandstone to the latter.	
4. Roofing slate, &c.	Submedial Order.	Transition Class.	Intermediate Class.
5. Mica, Gneiss, Granite, &c.	Inferior Order.	Primitive Class.	Primitive Class.

Primitive rocks may be considered as the foundation of all that we know of the covering of the earth. They are destitute of organic remains, and appear to have undergone few changes, which are supposed to have occurred before the existence of animals and vegetables. They are chiefly found in the central chains of great ranges of mountainous land, and generally form the foundation on which the other strata rest, though in them, as in every feature of geology, great irregularity is occasionally found.

The Secondary Formation, which rests on the Transition Class, is distinguished from the primary rocks by the presence of petrifactions in great number and variety. In this formation are included the extensive series of strata which form the coal measures, and also the carboniferous or mountain limestone of the lead-mining districts. The latter and its accompanying strata will be more minutely described in the following chapter. It may here be observed that the lead strata lie *under* the coal measures, and many who have visited Alston have been surprised on learning that the strata of its lofty hills lie, as regards geological position, under the deepest coal-mines of Newcastle. Particular details of the various formations named in the preceding table are contained in Conybeare and Phillips' Geology of England and Wales,—a work replete with plain and solid information, founded on actual observation, and entirely free from the flimsy and useless theories which have too long been the bane of this science.

Having thus briefly defined the general position of the strata in which the mines of Alston and its neighbourhood are worked, it may be observed that the proposed limits of these brief notices do not admit of more minute geological details. For the tourist and general reader enough space has probably been occupied on the subject. Those who desire to inquire more largely on these topics may find abundant sources of information in many geological works recently published. The Transactions of the London and Cornwall Geological Societies, and of the Cambridge Philosophical Society, furnish a copious fund of general information on this subject, and in the first volume of the Transactions of the Natural-History Society of Newcastle will be found some highly interesting papers and coloured sections, chiefly illustrative of the coal-fields. Occasional articles in the Quarterly and Edinburgh Reviews, * and various philosophical and scientific journals, are ever adding to the rapidly accumulating stores of information on geology. The third part of Williams' Mineral Kingdom contains much curious matter, from which readers of this class of works cannot but derive instruction blended with no small share of amusement. The author combines great practical knowledge with very confident theoretical notions, and describes the original formation and arrangement of the strata and mineral veins with a minuteness and decision more nearly resembling the style of an actual observer of the whole process, than that of a plausible though certainly most ingenious theorist.

* October 1830.

CHAP. IX.

STRATA OF THE MINING DISTRICTS.

Familiar Illustration of the Arrangement of Strata.— Rise and
Dip of Strata —General Division of Strata.— Grindstone Sill.
—Fell-top Limestone.—Coal.—Upper Coal Sill.—Upper and
Lower Slate Sills.—Firestone Sill. — Pattinson's Sill. — Little
Limestone.— Great Limestone.—Tuft.— Limestone Post.—
Quarry Hazel.—Girdle or Till Bed.—Four-fathom Limestone.
—Coal.— Nattrass Gill Hazel. —Three-yards Limestone.—
Six-fathom Hazel.—Five-yards Limestone.— Slaty Hazel.—
Scar Limestone. — Cockle-Shell Limestone. —Tyne-Bottom
Plate. —Tyne-Bottom Limestone. —Whetstone Bed.— Great
Whin Sill.

ROCKS or other mineral bodies lying successively in
layers upon each other, either horizontally or more or
less inclined to the horizon, are designated by the
terms *stratum* (plural *strata*). A number of quires of
brown, blue, and yellow paper in successive layers
form a humble model of stratification; and if a
few sheets of one colour, a quire of another, two or
three quires of another, and so on, be arranged alternately, so as to correspond with the various thicknesses
of the strata, they will form a tolerably correct model
of a section of strata in the mining districts. The blue
paper may represent limestone; the yellow, sandstone;
and the brown, slate beds or indurated clay. This
model would represent the strata of Alston, as it is
supposed they once existed, that is, without any undu-
lation of surface,—without hills, dales, rivers,—without
veins or any other of those numerous dislocations
which now exist. For, from the exact coincidence of

I

the strata on the opposite sides of valleys, it is inferred that they were once continuous, and that the hollowing of them, or the formation of valleys, was the result of subsequent changes on the surface of the globe.

Having thus obtained an idea of the position of the strata, in what may be supposed their original state, it may be observed that they now lie in an inclined position, which varies considerably, but on the line of the greatest acclivity forms an angle of about 2° 15′. The average bearing of this rise is 30° west of south from the true meridian. This inclination of the strata is very conspicuous on the sides of Ale Fell, opposite the turnpike road from Hexham to Alston. At a little distance above Clargill House, the great limestone is seen emerging from and forming the bed of the rivulet; from thence, with a gradual ascent marked by deep swallow-holes and by the limits of cultivated land, it climbs the mountainous brow of Ale Fell, and bassetts or crops out at the western extremity of the hill, after attaining a considerable elevation. This inclination of the strata is commonly known by the familiar terms of *rise* and *dip*.

In 1800, an engraved Section was published by W. Millar, Miner, of Carlisle, exhibiting the various succession of the strata, from the highest in Alston Moor to the lowest on the north-east side of the Keswick hills. Since that time, a Treatise on a Section of the Strata from Newcastle to the Mountain of Crossfell, by Westgarth Forster, has gone through two editions, the latter published in 1821. These, and engraved plans of Holyfield and Hudgill Cross-Vein Mines, with coloured sections of the strata and workings, published in 1828, by Dickinson and Sopwith, Surveyors, are the only publications relating solely to Alston Moor that the author is acquainted with.

The great limestone may be considered as dividing the strata of this district into two portions; the upper one consisting of alternate siliceous and argillaceous beds, with only two very thin beds of limestone, while the under portion contains several calcareous strata of considerable thickness. In the following notices of these several strata, some reference has been made to Mr. Forster's work, but for the greater portion of them the Editor has to express his obligation to Mr. John Leithart, of Alston, an intelligent mining agent, who has communicated several interesting particulars.

One of the highest of the siliceous strata is called grey millstone or greystone, a coarse stone, sometimes quarried for millstones. It appears on the mountains between Wolsingham and Stanhope, but does not occur near Alston. Though coarser, it resembles in character the lower part of the Nattrass Gill hazel.

The GRINDSTONE SILL is about four fathoms thick, and less porous and hard than the millstone. In some places it is hewn into grindstones, and is the highest stratum at Allenheads, Coalcleugh, and Rampgill: it is also nearly the highest stratum on Crossfell mountain. Near Alston, neither this stratum nor the grey millstone possesses any value in a mining point of view, but in Derwent some veins have been found to be productive in it.

The FELL-TOP LIMESTONE is the first or highest calcareous stratum that occurs in the mining district. Near Alston it is sometimes called *Tullas green limestone*, from its being at the surface of an allotment of that name on the summit of the mountainous range called Middle Fell. It contains magnesia, is of a laminated structure, and remarkable for the sonorous quality of the musical stones found in it, which are capable of producing various tones. It affords excellent lime, but is too thin to be of consequence in mining, seldom exceeding four or five feet.

Under this limestone is a thin seam of COAL, which, with most of the other seams in the district, is commonly called *crow coal*. It is of inferior quality, and is sold at about half the price of good coals, which are chiefly brought to Alston from Hartleyburn. In consuming, the crow coal emits sulphureous effluvia, and its flame is of various shades of blue and green. The broken portion of the seam near its bassett is frequently mixed with clay by trampling them together with the feet,—the mixture is then formed into round balls called *cats*, a useful, though homely fuel, which is used by the poorer classes.

The UPPER COAL SILL, a siliceous stratum so called, varies from one to two fathoms in thickness. Under it is a plate bed of considerable thickness, (from five to eight fathoms); and under this another hazel occurs of a close texture, used for sharpening scythes, and from thence called the WHETSTONE SILL. Its particles are hard and globular; but when angular particles are mixed with it, they render it unfit for use as a whetstone, either in a compact or a sandy state.

The UPPER AND LOWER SLATE SILLS are about four fathoms in thickness; their structure is a medium between the coarse and fine hazels, and is more laminated than any other in Alston Moor. These strata are very extensively quarried for roofing slates and flags in several parts of Alston Moor. They are commonly called *grey slate*, and form the massive covering of nearly all the houses in the neighbourhood. In mining they have not been productive of much lead, except at Rampgill vein, which, by its richness in nearly every stratum, forms an exception to the general nature of veins in the district.

The FIRESTONE SILL is a coarse siliceous stratum about six fathoms in thickness, similar in structure to the lower part of Nattrass Gill hazel. It is frequently quarried for fencing and building. Its colour is a reddish grey, and it is softer than most of the hazels. Both the earthy and the metallic contents of veins in traversing this stratum attain their maximum specific gravity, and in it also the sulphate of barytes is a more frequent component of mineral veins than in any other stratum in Alston Moor.

PATTINSON'S SILL lies from ten to twelve fathoms below the firestone, and derives its name from the person who first sunk into it at Rampgill vein. Its thickness is about two fathoms, and in structure it is hard and refractory. It is of a dull white colour streaked with black, and is frequently united with the girdle beds above, which occasions its variable thickness. Veins have often been productive in it, but it is seldom used for building purposes.

The LITTLE LIMESTONE is the second calcareous stratum of this mining field, lying about forty-six fathoms below the fell-top limestone, and from ten to twelve fathoms above the great limestone. It is a hard, impure, and brownish-blue-coloured limestone, of a contorted structure, about three yards thick, and has no regular flats in it. Many veins have been very productive in this stratum, and in general its metallic contents in traversing it are accompanied by few of the earthy minerals.

Between this stratum and the great limestone are two hazels called the *High and Low Coal Sills*, accompanied with thin seams of coal, mostly of inferior quality. The range of these strata may frequently be

3

discovered at a distance by the indications of the small coal workings along the sides of the hill where they crop out to the day.

The GREAT LIMESTONE is so called by way of pre-eminence, being the thickest limestone wrought in Alston Moor, and by far the most productive in mineral treasures.

This limestone, including the *tumbler* beds upon it, preserves a nearly uniform thickness of from nine to eleven fathoms. The tumblers are alternating beds or layers of limestone and famp beds, loose and confused in their arrangement, and in thickness about five yards. Between these and the main body of the limestone, is an earthy layer or famp bed, called the *black bed;* it is softer and darker than the other adjacent layers of a similar nature.

In the great limestone are three different flats, which are a certain horizontal disposition of the strata, the situation of which is well known in practical mining, but the nature of which is yet imperfectly understood. As they relate more to the veins than to the strata, some further notices of them will be given when describing the phenomena of veins. That portion of the great limestone called the high flat is about four feet below the black bed. From the high to the middle flat is about twelve feet, but the distance from this to the low flat varies from fourteen to twenty feet. These flats vary in thickness from one inch to six feet, and there have been instances, says Mr. Leithart, of all the flats being so thick at the same place as to form one whole mass of flat from the top of the high flat to the bottom of the undermost one. The subdivisions in this limestone are similar to those of the scar limestone, having one very thick post or layer about nine feet from the bottom of the stratum called the *thick post,* and usually from ten to thirteen feet in thickness. Immediately above it are a number of very thin posts from four to six inches in thickness. In the remainder of the limestone upwards, the subdivisions are somewhat regular, the posts or layers being from eighteen to thirty inches thick.

The TUFT or WATER SILL is a soft, dull-red-coloured siliceous stratum, lying immediately under the great limestone. It is about nine or ten feet thick, and contains much oxide of iron. Many veins that have been productive in the great limestone have also been productive in this. The tuft and the plate beds below it have not that distinct separating plane between them that usually marks the division of strata. The former gradually becomes more and more argillaceous and micaceous in its character until the quantities of silex, argil, and mica become nearly equal, forming what are termed, by miners, *grey beds,* about other nine or ten feet thick. The lower portion of these grey beds gradually blends with a plate bed nine or ten feet thick, and in this and the incumbent strata upwards to the great limestone, a vast proportion of the levels in this mining field are driven, owing to the easy access which they afford to the mine workings in the great limestone.

Below the plate bed is a thin stratum of impure limestone about eighteen inches thick. It is called the *limestone post,* and in sinking through it great inconvenience is often found from the quantity of water in it. It lies immediately on

The QUARRY HAZEL, a dull-red-coloured sandstone, somewhat harder and finer than the tuft, and containing a less proportion of mica. It varies in thickness from two to five fathoms. In some places it has been productive of lead, but not generally so. Mr.

Forster observes, that it is sometimes divided into two parts by a famp bed, but in general this famp bed lies at the bottom of the hazel, as the grey beds do at the bottom of the tuft. It would be desirable to have some definite idea of what constitutes the difference between grey beds and famp beds, as understood by miners, for at present the terms are often very vaguely applied. Mr. Leithart defines grey beds to be very thin beds of silex and argil in nearly equal proportions, or called hard or soft grey beds as these components more or less predominate. The term famp bed is applied to layers of variable thickness from a foot to a fathom, which are homogeneous, and have no regular divisions; they consist of mica, argil, and a little silex, and are always softer than the grey beds.

Beneath the quarry hazel is a plate bed from three to four fathoms in thickness, and under it lies the GIRDLE or TILL BED, a kind of chert bed sometimes divided into layers or posts, but more commonly homogeneous. Its colour is a brownish black, and it is much harder than any of the plate beds, but not so hard as the limestones. Veins that have been productive in the four-fathom limestone have also generally been so in the till bed, there being no intervening strata. The lower posts of the till bed and the upper ones of the four-fathom limestone occasionally have so close a resemblance that it is difficult to distinguish them. In thickness the till bed varies from three to five yards. Mr. Leithart observes that in this stratum he has generally found the metallic contents of veins pure and solid, that is, not much intermixed with the usual accompanying earthy minerals.

The FOUR-FATHOM LIMESTONE derives its name from its thickness, which it preserves more uniformly than any other stratum in Alston Moor. It does not possess the bright hue of the great and scar limestones, having a brown rusty appearance, and its bassett is unaccompanied with the external indications of swallow holes, which mark the course of the other limestones ; neither are there in it any flats, as in the great and the scar limestones. It contains much magnesia, especially the upper part, which is readily decomposed by exposure to the air.

This stratum is more equally divided into separate layers or beds than either the scar or the great limestone. The layers are from two to three feet in thickness, and are divided by perpendicular joints into regular rhomboidal blocks, and, when broken, the fragments more or less resemble this form.

Veins which have been productive in the great limestone have often proved less rich in lead in the four-fathom limestone, but they frequently contain a tolerable portion of the sulphuret of zinc, or, as it is here commonly called, *Black Jack.* The distance between the containing sides or cheeks of veins in this stratum is usually less than in the great and scar limestones. The prevailing mineral substance of veins in the four-fathom limestone is lime with oxide of iron, while, in the scar limestone, quartz, and in the great limestone, the carbonate of lime and fluate of lime, more frequently prevail. In general, mining operations in the four-fathom limestone are dry, owing to the free drainage caused by its numerous joints or fissures. Many workings, which in the incumbent strata have been flooded with water, have been completely drained immediately on reaching this limestone ; and this release from much expense and inconvenience is usually anticipated by miners. Many trials of veins have been made in this stratum, but they have not been generally productive ; and when they have been so, the ore has proved rich in lead, but poor in silver.

Under the four-fathom limestone is a seam of coal, which is not workable in any part of Alston Moor, except at Gilderdale Head and Hartside, where it is not of so sulphureous a quality as the coal generally is in the neighbourhood. Its average thickness is a foot, and it is principally used for burning lime, being much inferior to the Hartleyburn coal for household purposes. Immediately under this coal lies

The NATTRASS GILL HAZEL, a coarse, dull red-and-white-coloured stone. It is quarried on the road side near the first milestone from Alston on the Hexham road, and still more extensively at Nattrass Gill, from whence it takes its name. It is divided into two parts by a famp bed. Being the only stone in Alston Moor that admits of superior workmanship, it is much used for building, though, from its hardness, it is hewn with difficulty. In a mining point of view, no stratum is less important, veins in it being generally barren, and consequently few trials of any extent have been made in it. A considerable thickness of plate bed intervenes between the last-mentioned stratum and

The THREE-YARDS LIMESTONE, so called from its thickness in *some places,* in contradistinction to another lower limestone called in like manner the five-yards limestone. These appellations, however suitable to any particular mine, are very injudicious and incorrect when applied to a district; for, owing to the variable thickness of these, as of all strata, the three-yards limestone is in some places thicker than that which in name so much exceeds it.

The three-yards limestone is a pure, somewhat cavernous, and bright blue limestone, containing some organic remains. Few veins have been productive in it. Immediately under it lies

The SIX-FATHOM HAZEL, a fine, hard, and quartzy hazel, of a whitish colour. It makes good fences, but it is too hard to dress well, and consequently is not very suitable for building, yet the greater part of the town of Alston is built with it. Veins in it have not yet proved generally productive, but considerable trials have of late been made in it in different parts of the manor of Alston Moor.

The FIVE-YARDS LIMESTONE is an impure, flinty, dark-blue-coloured limestone, divided into numerous layers by thin argillaceous famp beds. Veins have not been found productive in it.

The SLATY HAZEL is coarse and laminated, from whence it derives its name. It is frequently called the Gossop-gate hazel, from having been extensively quarried for building purposes at a place of that name. It is in no way remarkable, and very few veins have been found productive in it.

The SCAR LIMESTONE is in thickness inferior only to the great limestone in this manor, being from five to nine fathoms. Its name is derived from the bold precipitous face which it so frequently presents, and which forms in many parts of the district a picturesque and romantic feature. In some instances, this precipitous bassett continues without interruption for more than a mile in length. At Nentforce and Eshgill, it appears in a remarkably interesting manner, and occasions the waterfalls of which mention has already been made. The tumblers at the top of it are about five yards in thickness, and the remainder is nearly pure limestone. In these tumblers there are two or more argillaceous chert beds, the high one being fifteen inches thick, the low one twenty inches, and the others, when they occur, are very thin, being only two or three inches in thickness.

In the scar limestone there are three flats. The highest is situated in a bed of limestone about five feet thick, between the two chert beds above named, and which is called by miners the *high flat post*. From the bottom of the low chert bed the limestone, for five feet in thickness, is composed of thin beds of limestone called the top posts. After these is the thick post, from ten to thirteen feet thick, in which both the middle and the low flats are situated, being separated about three feet. Under this is the bottom post, about six feet thick.

Veins have not been found very productive in this stratum, but when so, have produced more lead in flats than in perpendicular veins.

At Scarends, near Garrigill, the bassett of the scar limestone presents a continuous precipitous face for above one hundred yards in length, and in this natural section the limestone in the situation of the flats has a different character and stratum from what it has above and below, exhibiting a cavernous appearance, while the contiguous limestone upon and under the flats is of a more laminated and close texture.

Wherever the scar limestone is the surface stratum, the soil is of the richest quality in the district, producing very abundant crops of grass; and the line of its bassett, like that of the great limestone, is characterized by numerous funnel-like hollows or swallow holes, which occur in the tumbler beds, and do not enter the main body of the limestone. No limestones in this part of the country are accompanied by these holes, except this and the great limestone; neither are any other calcareous strata overlaid by the alternate beds of limestone and famp beds that constitute the tumblers.

A great number of thin alternating beds of hazel, plate, &c. lie under the scar limestone, and are exposed to observation in Nentforce Level. Among them is a thin bed of limestone, which, from the conspicuous appearance of its fossil contents, is called the COCKLE-SHELL LIMESTONE : these consist of entrochi, anomia, ostrea, and other organic remains. Between this and the next stratum of limestone, a number of thin beds of plate, grey beds, &c. occur. One of them is called the TYNE-BOTTOM PLATE, and is extremely hard, being of a closer and more laminated structure than any other plate bed in Alston Moor. The bridge at Garrigill Gate rests upon it. This plate bed first crops out at Beldy, near Garrigill, where it is thrown up by the Tyne-bottom great vein and several smaller veins, and has an acclivity which here forms an angle of 20° with the horizon. From thence to Tynehead House, a distance of three and a half miles, this stratum forms a precipitous face on each side of the Tyne nearly equal to its thickness, which is about three fathoms. The metallic contents of veins in this stratum are generally dense and pure, accompanied with few earthy minerals, except a rider formed by an incorporation of iron with the plate. Under this bed is the lowest calcareous stratum in Alston Moor, which is called

The TYNE-BOTTOM LIMESTONE, from its forming the bed of the South Tyne River for four miles above the village of Garrigill Gate. It is a hard, flinty, dark-blue-coloured limestone, contorted in structure, and about four fathoms thick. It contains three flats. A vein may be seen crossing this stratum a little below Garrigill bridge, and further down the river it presents some phenomena, which are highly interesting either to the scientific or to the general observer.

K

The above form the series of strata which, with great uniformity, extend over the important mining district of Alston Moor. For the interests of mining, it is to be regretted that they have not been subjected to minute and careful scientific research. A chemical analysis of the various strata, and of the contents of mineral veins contiguous to each, would be a valuable acquisition to science, and might in time afford some insight into the inexplicable uncertainties which now harass and impede mining operations. Some illustrations of this subject will, it is to be trusted, be found in the transactions of our local Natural-History Society.

Under the series of strata above described, a curious geological feature appears in a stratified range of basaltic rock. This is locally called the GREAT WHIN SILL, and is very conspicuous in the moors adjoining the early course of the rivers Tyne and Tees. It is extremely variable in thickness, being only four fathoms at Hilton in Westmoreland, from seven to eight fathoms at Dufton, at Silverband in Teesdale, it is twenty, and at Cauldron Snout, a waterfall on the Tees, nearly thirty fathoms. At Tyne-bottom mine, near Garrigill, says Mr. Forster, it is sunk into nearly twenty fathoms, and at Settlingstones lead-mines, near Haydon Bridge, it occurs at the surface, and is penetrated to the depth of twenty-two fathoms.

The insertion of basaltic or whin rock between layers of regular strata for a considerable distance, is a circumstance which has excited considerable attention. Williams, who, it has already been hinted, advances his opinions both with confidence and plausibility, strongly opposes the Plutonist theories of Dr. Hutton, and insists that basalt is "not a lava, but a real stone. There are," he continues, "in several places many and extensive strata of this stone, which are disposed in their stations among other strata of different characters and qualities, which are placed above and below the several strata of basalt; and these strata of basalt spread out as wide and stretch as far every way as the other different strata among which they are ranged." "I would ask Dr. Hutton," adds our author, "how he is to lift up the superincumbent strata to a sufficient and equal height from the strata below, for many miles extent every way, and to keep them asunder until such a quantity of melted lava is poured in as will fill up all the extensive empty space to form the new-inserted stratum." Williams refers, in proofs of his views of the subject, to the fact of "a considerable number of strata of basalt blended *stratum super stratum* among various other strata, among which are many seams of pit coal, and some of these coals are in immediate contact with strata of basalt, forming the immediate roof and floor of the coals, and these, with their concomitant strata, stretch for many miles.— Similar phenomena exist in West Lothian, in Ayrshire, Fife, &c." *

The volcanic origin of the WHIN SILL of Alston Moor, Teesdale, &c. is now generally considered as an established geological fact; and the theory of Williams, that such rocks were regularly deposited in the same manner as the stratified series, is no longer admitted in the creed of most geologists. The term of *whin sill* is objected to by Professor Sedgewick, because *sill* indicates a regular stratification of this rock, which he, with much acute reasoning, endeavours to disprove. Two highly-interesting papers in the second volume of the Cambridge Philosophical Transactions, by this able geologist, contain much valuable information on

* Williams' Mineral Kingdom.

the subject, being written expressly on the phenomena of the trap rocks in Yorkshire and Durham, and the geology of High Teesdale.

The insertion of basaltic rocks among the regular strata at Teesdale is a fact open to the observation of every eye at the waterfall of High Force. In the mine of Silverband, nearly two miles higher up the Tees, the author has descended a shaft sunk through regular strata to the whin sill, *in which* the miners were then *raising lead ore*. The superincumbent strata here are considered to correspond with those which rest on the whin sill at Alston.

Miners generally are shrewd and observing, and their interest is closely interwoven with a knowledge of the strata, veins, &c., which indeed is forced upon them by their occupation. The author has had many opportunities of hearing the discussions of these *practical geologists,* who, though unacquainted with the technical language of science and the abstruse theories of the learned, possess an ample knowledge of many remarkable facts, which, if collected, would be of great advantage to science. These conversations are chiefly confined to themselves, and, however interesting, are for the most part doomed to " waste their sweetness on the desert air." An able reporter, concealed so as to hear the discussions of a company of miners assembled in a tavern, would often obtain information expressed with a clearness and energy which might in vain be sought for in the formal investigations of scientific inquiry.

CHAP. X.

MINERAL VEINS.

Comparative Magnitude of Veins.—Various Names of Veins.—
Prior Formation of Veins or Cross Veins.—Hade and Throw
of Veins.—Contents of Mineral Veins.—Great Sulphur
Vein.—Spar.—Galena.—Silver.—Copper.—Slip Vein.—
Gash Vein.—Flats.

————

HAVING, in the preceding chapter, supposed successive
layers of different coloured paper to afford an idea of
the strata in the mining districts, and confined our
description to these strata only; we come now to
describe the other features which accompany that
arrangement. The undulating surface of the country
presents a great variety of these strata bassetting or
cropping out on the inclined surface of the hills, which
corresponding hollows cut in the model, or layers of
paper, would very aptly represent. But with this exception, that the great mass of strata is not, like the
layers of paper, uniform in inclination, but subject to
many varieties of position, some of them abrupt and
unaccountable. The principal of these varieties are
caused by veins traversing the strata, and containing
more or less of metallic ores. These veins may be
briefly defined as greater or less cracks in the crust of
the earth, and are comparatively not greater in proportion to the mass of the strata in the districts intersected by them, than the minute cracks which would
be found in a small clay model of the district when
drying. In all speculations of this kind, we must con-
stantly remember the relative proportion which the
human race bears to the gigantic fabric of the earth,

3

which cannot be more effectually done than by reducing both to a scale easily comprehended. Alston Manor, represented by a model in clay, on a scale of two inches to a mile, would be about fourteen inches square. The annexed sketch represents the veins of Hudgill

Burn Mine drawn to this scale, from which it will be seen that the comparative size and position of these celebrated veins have the same proportion to the surrounding country as the small cracks have to the model described at page 77.

Most veins in the mining district preserve a tolerably direct course for a considerable distance, some, indeed, for several miles. They are commonly designated *veins, cross veins*, and *quarter-point veins*. The former are sometimes called *right-running veins*, and have a direction or bearing approaching nearly to east and west, and slightly varying from that to a northeast and south-west direction. Those which have a bearing nearly north and south are called *cross veins*. Nearly all the veins in the mining districts come under one or other of these denominations. The few veins which have a bearing between these are, on that account, called *quarter-point veins*. The "point" of a vein is the usual phrase to designate its bearing.

Another distinction in the general name of veins arises from their relative situation, as follows. If three east and west veins lie near each other, the middle one is simply designated by its particular name, as, for instance, Hudgill Burn Vein; the vein north of this is called Hudgill Burn North Vein, and that to the south, Hudgill Burn Sun Vein,—*sun*, in mining phraseology, being invariably used for south. If more veins lie nearly parallel, they are sometimes, as at Hudgill Burn, denominated the Second Sun Vein, or Third Sun Vein, according to their relative situation. The particular names of veins, both in Alston and the adjoining districts, are for the most part derived from those of the estates, farms, or other conspicuous objects in or near which they have been chiefly worked, though in some few instances they have been called after the names of individuals, and in others received their designation from mere caprice.

Cross Veins, when near together, are distinguished by the names of East and West Cross Veins. It may be observed, that the names of veins do not extend to their whole course, but only to a limited extent; thus, for instance, Sir John's Vein, Stowcrag Vein, Scarends Vein, Leehouse Well Vein, &c., are all one continued cross vein in different portions of its length. High Coal Cleugh Vein, in Allendale manor, continues westward into Alston Moor, where it takes the name of Rampgill. On crossing the river Nent, it is called Brigill Burn Vein, and afterwards Browngill Vein, &c.—these names being, in most instances, limited to what is called a *lease length*, which, in Alston Moor, is usually about 1200 yards.

Much ingenuity has been exercised on the theory of *veins*, and it seems established from very conclusive evidences, that all the strata have undergone very important changes, among which are to be numbered the formation of veins. After observing that the

greater part of veins approximate either to an east and
west or to a north and south bearing, and consequently
cross at nearly right angles, the next circumstance that
deserves attention is the fact that the cross veins usually preserve a continued course, while east and west
veins at their intersection are very frequently carried
off their point, being removed farther north or south,
and then pursuing their former direction.   From this
phenomenon arises a frequent query, whether cross
veins, or east and west veins, are of prior formation.
As far as argument is concerned, much has been advanced on both sides of the question.   Werner's opinion
is as follows : — " By the crossing and intersecting of
veins, the antiquity or relative age of each *can be
easily assigned.*   Every vein which intersects another
is newer than the one traversed, and is of later formation than all those which it traverses.   This crossing
of veins is of great importance, and deserves to be kept
in remembrance by all who wish to become acquainted
with the study of veins; yet, till very lately, it has
always escaped the observation of mineralogists."   On
the other hand, practical mining exhibits a seeming
refutation of this doctrine.   " Cross veins," says a
highly intelligent miner, speaking on the subject, " I
suppose to be fissures, which were first formed, and
this easily accounts for the shifting of east and west
veins, by supposing the force which created these
second veins not strong enough to carry them directly
through the cross vein, but yet sufficient to continue
the fissure in the next weakest place.   The Wernerian
system (he continues) seems absurd, because if the
east and west veins were first formed, it would require
the whole strata to be shifted along with them, which
alone could carry them off their point, besides which,
while one vein is carried off its point northward, ano-

ther lying near it is removed southward, whereas, if a longitudinal shift of the strata occurred at the formation of the cross vein, all the other veins would be removed in one direction." Nor is this general rule of cross veins intersecting east and west veins without exceptions, as Scaleburn Cross Vein, at Nenthead in Alston Moor, is carried eighty feet off its point by an east and west vein.

What chiefly bewilders all speculations on these subjects, is our utter inability to form any but very limited ideas even of a small portion of a district, far less of a kingdom, or any material extent of the earth's surface. The eye of man, as far as geology is concerned, is powerfully microscopic, and many of the theories which have been advanced, too much resemble the supposed speculations of the fly on St. Paul's Cathedral, which Addison describes as condemning the architect for the roughness and irregular surface of that structure. Whether veins were formed by a gradual drying of the strata of the earth, or by some sudden convulsion of nature, we cannot determine; but in either case, conflicting powers, of which we can form no adequate conception, may have caused the various features which perplex the geologist, and baffle all attempts to form a clear and uniform system. In the present question, the fact of east and west veins being often split on approaching, and then entirely lost in a cross vein, seems an almost conclusive evidence that the ruined vein is newer than that which has caused its destruction. Accumulated evidence placed in a clear and tangible form can alone throw light on this and many other phenomena of mineral veins.

The HADE of veins is the mining term for that inclination which nearly all veins have from a perpendicular direction. Thus a vein is said to hade to the

north when it inclines further north as it deepens. In
Weardale the veins mostly hade to the south, and in
Allendale and Alston in the contrary direction. This
hade or inclination is not in one uniform direction,
but varies with the strata, being nearer a perpendicular direction in hard strata, and considerably more
inclined in plate beds, and its direction sometimes
varies in the same vein. The upper side of a hading
vein is commonly called the hanging cheek, or, more
briefly, "the hanger." The under side is named the
ledger cheek or "ledger."

The hade of veins is often of great consequence
when the course of a vein runs at a little distance from
and parallel with the boundary of another manor or
estate, of which a singular instance occurred in Weardale about fifteen years ago. A freehold estate of 30
or 40 acres was purchased for £ 1500. A vein leased
by Mr. Jopling, under the Dean and Chapter of Durham, ran parallel with, and at a short distance from,
one of the boundaries of the purchase; but the vein
hading into the royalty of the said estate, the proprietor received from Mr. Jopling one-fifth duty, which
amounted in all to about £ 800.

The THROW of veins is the usual mining term for
that vertical disruption of the strata which very generally occurs near veins of any considerable magnitude,
and is represented in Fig. 1, page 77. This perpendicular distance between the corresponding strata on
the opposite sides of a vein, varies from a few inches
to thirty or forty fathoms, and in some instances to a
hundred fathoms. There is a remarkable correspond-
ence between the hade and throw of veins, to which,
though not without exceptions, the following rule
applies in Alston Moor.

If an east and west vein throws the strata up on the south side of the vein, then the hade of that vein is to the north, and the contrary strata are thrown up on the north side, and so of all other veins. The hade is usually opposite the side on which the strata are highest, or, in other words, the strata are highest on the ledger side of the vein. The following is a curious instance of the variable throw of veins. Old Carr's Cross Vein, in Alston Moor, in mining language, is *weakest* at the north end, and increases in *strength* northwards. This powerful vein throws up the strata,

At Middle Cleugh Second Sun Vein, 42 feet.
At Middle Cleugh Vein, ... 48 —
At Carr's Vein, ... 60 —
At Broomsberry, ... 72 —
At Nentsberry Greens, ... 162 —

It is easy to imagine how, when the strata were separated by the formation of veins, some portions should sink, or others be raised from the level they occupied before; but it is not so easy to account for the fact, that, however great may be the vertical disruption of the strata, no trace of it appears on the surface; for when the strata are removed a distance of one or two hundred feet, it would be reasonable to suppose that some lofty precipice on the surface would betoken the mighty rent. Such, however, is not the case, and to offer reasons to account for it, seems but a waste of words. It is yet among the hidden mysteries of that mysterious agency which has effected this and other changes in the mineral kingdom.

But by far the most important and interesting feature connected with the veins of a mining district are their mineral contents, and especially those subterranean treasures, in the pursuit of which so much capital, labour, and ingenuity have been for many centuries expended, and which have furnished so important and valuable produce for the service of mankind.

Williams, the author of the Natural History of the Mineral Kingdom, who, in the course of a professional experience of forty years, had many opportunities of acquiring the most minute information respecting mineral veins, enumerates and describes the following contents of veins:—Rider or vein stone, calcareous spar, cauk spar, quartzy spar, druse, white mineral soil, red fatty clay, bluish and greenish mineral soils, yellowish ash-coloured and marbled soft soils, black and blackish-brown soft soils, and brown mineral soil.

His detailed description of these would exceed the limits proposed in this brief account of the mining districts, and scarcely be of any interest to the general reader.

In Alston the contents of the unproductive parts of veins are chiefly described in mining phrase, as *dowk* and *rider*. The former is a brown, friable, and soft soil; the latter a hard stony matter, varying much in colour, hardness, and other characteristics. *Veinstone* is the more appropriate name given to it by Williams. In the Alston mines it is frequently mixed or marbled with white and other variously-coloured minerals, the whole forming a compact rocky substance. The rider of veins in limestone strata is generally of a dark grey colour, and sometimes black. A remarkable feature, which has often attracted the attention of the writer of these notices, is the almost incontestible evidence of the agency of fire in mineral veins, many portions of which exhibit either the appearance of having been actually burnt, or an extremely close resemblance to it. Few shareholders of mines are strangers to the terms thus briefly described; and as the firmness of the *dowk* and certain favourable appearances of the *rider* in veins are often considered to be indications of the vicinity of ore, the news of "*bonny dowk*" and "*excellent rider*" have frequently proved the only solace of unsuccessful adventurers, whose nearly exhausted patience, revived by these slender threads of hope, has again been roused into perseverance.

The rider of some strong veins, says Forster, is so remarkably hard as to resist the action of the atmosphere, while the adjoining strata have, to a certain extent, been removed by this constant and powerful agency; an instance of this occurs along the course of the great sulphur vein at Nunstones, near Tynehead. The summit of this hill is marked by conspicuous rocky stones, observable at a considerable distance; but these must have been prominent objects from a very remote period, if their name of *Nun*-stones bears the same antiquity as that of *Priors*-dale, the name of the district.

It may here be remarked, that Nunstones Great Copper Vein, (or, as it was denominated in a lease, "*the back bone of the earth*"), is the largest and strongest vein in Alston. Where it passes Crossgill Burn, it is no less than *three hundred feet* in width, and throws up the strata *eighty feet*. It contains much amorphous white quartz, several strong ribs of sulphur, and some yellow copper ore. Trials have, of late years, been made in this vein by the Commissioners of Greenwich Hospital, but without much success. A shaft was sunk from the middle of the scar limestone to the Tyne-bottom plate, a depth of nearly one hundred and fifty feet. John Taylor, Esq., of London, a gentleman of great eminence and acknowledged skill in mining affairs, describes this vein rather as a collection of branches than one single continued vein, and supposes that copper to a considerable amount may probably be

L

obtained from it, especially where it intersects the
continuation of Stowcrag vein. In this latter vein
Mr. Taylor viewed a rich deposit of copper ore, which
considerably increased his hopes as to the existence
and value of copper ores in the Alston district.

The beautiful spars which adorn the mantel-pieces
of many houses in the northern towns are often designated by the general name of Alston Moor spars. But
only a very small proportion of them are the product
of veins in this manor, by far the most beautiful and
abundant of these specimens being found in the
mines of Weardale and Allendale. Fluor spar of
different colours, quartz, and the ore of zinc, blend and
calamine, or *Black Jack*, as it is locally termed, are the
prevailing spars of Alston Moor, and are usually claimed as a perquisite by the miners, by whom they are
sold. In the town of Alston are several mineral shops,
where not only the spars of the district, but many
others from a distance, are exposed for sale.

Of those minerals which are the especial objects of
the miner's search, and constitute the subterranean
wealth of the district, GALENA, *(Glance bleiglanz*, of
Werner), from which is produced the well-known LEAD
of commerce, is by far the most abundant. The colour
and mineral aspect of this ore are so familiar to
every one, as to require no description here. The specific gravity of galena is from 7 to 7·6, and the proportion of lead contained in it varies from 40 to 85
per cent. The ores of Alston generally approach the
latter. The author was informed by an intelligent
smelting agent in Teesdale, that he never knew an
instance of galena entirely unmixed with silver, but
the proportion is frequently so small as not to repay
the expense of refining. When more than six or seven
ounces of silver can be produced from a fother of lead

(21 cwt.), it is refinable for the market; but the ores of Alston vary from a content of little or no silver, to as high a quantity as 93 ounces per fother, an extraordinary produce, and more than quadruple the produce of what are considered tolerably rich silver ores. The ores of Hudgill Burn Mine, in 1821, produced on the average about 13 ounces per fother, which amounted during that year to upwards of 32,000 ounces, worth, at 5s. 3d. per ounce, £ 8400.

From assays made at various times, from thirty to fifty years ago, the silver produce of some of the principal mines is stated as follows:—

	oz.	dwt.
Thortergill Vein, - - -	21	5
Nentsberry Hags, - -	20	18
Windy Brow, - - - -	17	12
Rampgill, - - - - -	9	6
Brownley Hill North Vein,	8	1
Blagill, - - - - -	7	7
Carr's Vein, - - - -	4	13

Ores rich in silver are generally bright and shining, while poor ores produce more iron. According to some, the component parts of Galena consist of lead, sulphur, carbonated lime, and oxide of iron; the various quantities of each analysis doubtless arising from the various quality of the ores examined. The following is the result of Dr. Thomson's experiments:—

Lead - - -	85·13
Sulphur - -	13·02
Oxide of Iron -	·5
	98·65
Loss - - -	1·35
	100·

The carbonate of lead has been found but sparingly in Alston Moor. It is remarkable for being nearly white, and consists of oxide of lead, carbonic acid, and water.

Yellow copper ore, which has been found in Stow-crag mine, adjoining the southern boundary of this manor, has not yet been produced in any considerable quantities in this manor. The author had the pleasure of viewing at Leehouse Well, a few years ago, the most splendid specimen of a copper vein that has ever been known in the manor, or probably in the north of England. The level for trial of the vein was by a singular chance driven into a remarkably rich deposit of copper pyrites, which extended over the top and sides of the level for above three feet in width, as well as over the forehead. The brilliant effect imparted by a number of lights on so large an extent of spark-ling yellow ore was extremely imposing, and the novelty of the scene and the brightness of the colours rendered it highly interesting.

Williams, in his " Mineral Kingdom," enumerates four different species of mineral veins. " The rake vein or perpendicular mineral fissure ; the pipe vein ; the flat or dilated vein ; and the accumulated vein. The rake vein (he adds) is the most common and best known among practical miners. Its origin and natu-ral cause are the same as the slips or dikes in the coal-mines." Thus what in the coal-mines disarranges the regular course of the coal, and is the frequent source of great perplexity and expense, forms in the mining districts the only situation in which lead ore can be obtained. Williams divides the rake vein into two classes. One, which he calls the slip vein, is that which commonly prevails in Alston Moor, and its chief characteristic is, that the strata on each side do not coincide, but one side is thrown higher than the other, as has already been described. This throw or slip he attributes to the escape of water during the formation of the strata, by the weight of the accumulations upon them. Caverns, he supposes, were thus formed, whereby a portion of the incumbent strata fell, and left its corresponding side more or less high, according to the depth of the chasm. The space between the sides of this fissure formed slip veins. The second class of veins, Williams calls "gash veins," which are open fissures narrowing as they deepen. The account of pipe and accumulated veins, in the "Mineral Kingdom," is well worth perusal; but they do not exist in the manor now described, and the author wishes chiefly to limit his description to what he has personally observed. Extended details are better suited for the materials of a copious volume, than the brief limits of a pocket tour-book. *Flat Veins*, or as in Alston they are more commonly termed "*flats*," are however too important an accompaniment of veins in this manor to be passed unnoticed.

Veins in general are very far from preserving a regular width, either in their height or length. In the former they are often affected by the strata, being compressed into narrow bounds in siliceous strata, and extended to a considerably greater width in limestone. So also lengthways they are subject to narrowings or *twitches*, and to wide and sometimes very extensive openings called *bellies* or caverns. The former perplex and disappoint the miner, who knows not how far these twitches may continue, producing a disappointment like that which is caused by a slip in a coal-mine. The veins in Alston Moor do not contain any of those extensive and splendid caverns which Williams describes in such glowing terms, but of which some specimens exist in the adjoining manors of Allendale and Weardale. Some of the flats in the Alston mines, however, present a magnificent spectacle. Small-cleugh Flats, at Nenthead, have been rich in ore for many years, but are now less productive. They are so easy of access that ladies can visit them, without encountering the usual obstacles of a mining excursion. The ore in these flats (as the name implies) lies hori-zontally, and the excavations in them are several yards in breadth. The sides in many places are encrusted with spar, and the whole seldom fails to interest the visitor, though it affords no clear idea of the usual modes of obtaining ore in veins.

Veins usually have cheeks, which, however irregular in width, still preserve the character of a fissure; but in certain parts of some strata, especially in the great and scar limestones, a vein branches off laterally into *flats,* which are often very productive of ore, as, for instance, those of Smallcleugh. These flats vary as much in their size and nature as veins; sometimes no lateral extension of a vein occurs at those parts of the strata where only flats occur. Sometimes the miners, when in the region of the flats, discover caverns of various extent, from a nut-shell to several feet; these contain more or less of spar, rider, clay, &c. A lateral opening often terminates in a wedge-like form from the vein, and here, in mining language, the vein is said to *find ease,* and in these places often produces much ore. Flats occasionally reach to a great extent like a regular stratum, and terminate suddenly by a *back* or joint in the strata, and not in wedge-like shape. A flat of this kind was recently worked by the London Lead-Company, and, after producing a consi-derable quantity of ore, was terminated in this manner.

Whether the structure of the stratum is different at the *random* or level of the flats is scarcely known. Mr. Leithart states that, in the interior of mines, the strata adjoining the flats are hard and compact, and *seem* no way different from the general body of limestone ; yet the same observing and experienced miner is of opinion that there exists, at the random of the flats, a certain peculiar structure, which he has seen developed at the basset of the scar limestone, near Scarends mine. Flats have for some years been worked very extensively at Holyfield mine, near the town of Alston. They are in some places of considerable width, and accompanied by numerous strings running obliquely through the vein. Sometimes a flat, when separated from a large vein, has numerous strings or *leaders* running into it; the latter term is applied by miners, because, by following them, they are often led to the flats.

Finally, in this very brief and imperfect description of lead veins, let it be our hope that numerous stores are yet existing, to be for ages brought forth in plenteousness, productive alike of wealth to the adventurer and comfort to the miner. And whoever has a share of patriotic feeling in his breast, cannot but earnestly hope that the produce of our native mines may speedily obtain such a remunerating price, as may relieve the mining districts from that distress which now, like a dark and threatening cloud, hangs heavily upon them.

CHAP. XI.

LEAD MINES.

Progress of Mining.—Old Method of working Mines.—Nentforce Level.—Ventilation of Mines. — Discovery of Hudgill Burn Mine. — Present Mode of working Mines. — Mine Shops. — Visit to a Lead Mine.

———

THE "sweet influence of the stars" is no longer studied as a subterranean guide, and the miner has ceased from wandering in search of hidden treasures with a hazel or apple-tree stick in his hand. Utterly absurd as this doctrine of the *Virgula Divina* appears to be, it is not perhaps generally known that so late as the year 1778 its efficiency in discovering veins was believed and asserted by an able and experienced writer on the Cornish mines. Pryce, in a large folio volume, including a vast fund of information on practical mining, devotes eleven pages and a plate to illustrate the various properties of the "magical rod," which, however, has long been disused, nor indeed are there any records of its having ever been used in the district of which we now treat.

Few and simple are the annals of mining, and centuries have left only meagre traces of the history of the secluded districts in which it has chiefly flourished. A few memorials of successive charters evince the importance of the mines upwards of six hundred years ago. From thence a period of four hundred years passed over, when the almost boundless treasures of this extensive mining field were supposed to be exhausted. (See p. 24.) Another century and a half is almost, if not entirely, barren of any interesting information on the mines,—the "memory of man" from time to time has been the only historical record of the mining operations of Alston Moor.

Separated from the rest of the world so much as these districts have until lately been, it is probable that the early processes of mining were rude and simple, and if not tinctured with superstition, at least cramped with idle and pernicious theories. So late as sixty years ago, a current opinion prevailed that a judgment of veins might be formed from the nature of the surface and the uppermost stratum. Under clay and moss lying on a limestone, a vein was considered likely to be productive in limestone; and where a hazel stratum was covered by hard, firm ground, the vein passing through that part was to be rich only in hazel strata. If clay and hazel, or firm ground and limestone, united at the surface, the miner anticipated a less fortunate result. But these visionary conceits have long been discarded in practical mining.

The old method of working mines was chiefly by means of shafts sunk into the vein, and, when necessary, levels were driven to drain the water. The work was brought along the drifts by boys, and drawn up the shafts in kibbles or small tubs by a *whimsey* or roller, worked by men or horses, according to the extent of the mine. In very large mines, the principal or day shaft was called the horse whimsey, while men or boys raised the ore up the successive *sumps,* * which communicated with the deep workings. The water levels were made so as merely to admit the workmen, and were from 4 to 5 feet high, 2 feet wide near the top, and from 15 to 18 inches at the bottom. Though called *levels,* their inclination often varied with the

---

* The mining term for a shaft in the interior of a mine.

strata, and they sometimes rose so much as the rapid
ascent of 45°.   Smeaton, the celebrated engineer, was
for three years one of the Receivers of the Greenwich
Hospital Estates, and, had he not been required in more
important pursuits, it is probable that the mines would
have derived great advantages from his talents.

The aqueduct of Nentforce Level was projected
and commenced under the direction of Smeaton, and,
though it has not yet produced the results he anticipated, the sound judgment and propriety of the design
are generally allowed.   The undertaking has not yet
reached the most productive part of the manor at
Nenthead, where it is probable that this adventurous
and stupendous work may open out a world of wealth
in a new and deep mining field.   Whatever the *future*
advantages of Nentforce Level may be, it has already
been the means of introducing great improvements in
the practice of mining.   Among these is the general
use of horse levels, by which an easy access is gained
to the mines.   The work is brought out with great
facility, and the health of the miners preserved by the
improved ventilation thus obtained.   This superior mode
of working mines is said to have been first introduced
into the country by Sir Walter Calverly Blackett,
about the year 1760, but was not generally adopted
for many years.   Again, Nentforce Level set the example of cast-iron railways, which, in the London
Lead Company's works and numerous other mines,
were speedily adopted in the place of wood rails.

Mr. Smeaton, when receiver, surveyed the workings
of Rampgill vein to decide the boundary between
Alston and Allendale Manors ; and the amazing value
of that important vein well deserved the inquiries of so
able an engineer.   It is not improbable that the powerful mind of Smeaton, and the effective works planned

by him, gave a stimulus to mining; for, since that period, both practical skill and a spirit of adventure have rapidly increased. In 1780, Messrs. Walton and Co. bought a mine at Nenthead for £ 205, and, being fortunate here, they engaged in other subterranean adventures in Alston, and thus commenced a new era in mining. Many new companies soon after commenced either the trial of veins or the re-working of old mines, and, among others, two families in humble circumstances began in the year 1782 to work in Farnberry vein, which was supposed to be exhausted. These adventurers proceeded with great industry to explore the old workings, and the success which rewarded their exertions induced other working miners to enter on similar undertakings. Up to this period, mines had been worked only by capitalists, but now many miners work the amount of their shares, while other partners contribute their funds; and trials of this kind have frequently been productive of considerable profit. One miner, without either money or education, gained £ 8000 in a few years by mining adventure, and many instances of more or less good fortune have occurred, though not unmixed with a share of those disappointments which, in mining as in every other pursuit, are the appointed lot of man.

The ventilation of extensive mines has been gradually improved at different periods, and by various means. Tin pipes were first used by Lord Carlisle and Co. at Tyne-bottom mine; Mr. Stagg introduced iron pipes at Rampgill; and Mr. Thomas Dickinson, the present agent or Moor Master of Alston, has made use of lead pipes for the same purpose in ventilating Nentforce Level. The first of these materials was found to decay speedily, but both it and the others are great improvements on the wooden boxes formerly in

use.   These not only rendered the air impure, but
could not be made air-tight.   Lead is indeed the most
costly, but it is also the most durable, and most useful
when taken out.

In 1796, an improved mode of washing ores was
introduced by Richard Trathen, a Cornish miner, who
came in search of employment, and proposed to obtain
considerable quantities of ore from the refuse of the
then inexperienced washers.   A stamp mill was erected
at the cost of the London Lead Company, who employed him, and Trathen fulfilled his engagements.
In a little time, Trathen's *bargain* per ton produced
him such good wages, that the agent endeavoured to
reduce them ; but the attempt was steadily resisted.
Trathen was therefore dismissed, and a whole summer
passed in the fruitless efforts of others to supply his
place.   He was again employed, and continued in
the company's service until prevented by age and
infirmity.   His sons supported him till his death, and
have since continued to follow the same business under
the company.

A few years after Trathen's arrival, another important improvement was introduced into Alston by Mr.
Utrick Walton, a respectable and successful miner.
This was the crushing mill, which now forms so conspicuous an object in the washing floors of large mines.
The circumstances connected with the introduction of
the mill not only exemplify the nature of mining, but
form a curious illustration how much experience and
judgment may be exercised in it.   Mr. Walton *selected*
a vein which proved worthy of trial, he *pursued* it
under discouraging circumstances until rewarded by
its treasures, and he had either the sound judgment or
the good fortune to leave it when it was no longer
worth possessing.   The particulars are these.   Mr.

Walton, in returning from a mine to his residence at the Nest, near Alston, discovered in a burn a vein which had been laid bare by a recent thunder shower, and on the same day he applied to the Moor Master for leave to try it, which was soon after granted. Mr. W.'s partners at another mine declined joining in this adventure, and he therefore prosecuted the trial at his own risk. He drove a level towards the vein at an expense of about £ 1200, but in three or four years a rich vein rewarded his perseverance, which in one year not only defrayed all the previous cost, but also produced a clear profit of upwards of £ 1000. After working the mine with success for several years, Mr. W. took up the rails, sold them with the crushing mill and other appendages, and bade a long farewell to what he deemed no longer worth pursuing.

This crushing mill, after being used several years, was sold for exactly the sum which it cost when new. An engraving of one of these mills is given in Forster's Section of the Strata, accompanied with a minute description, which precludes the necessity of any lengthened description here. The general reader will best understand its utility and mode of operation from a comparison with a coffee-mill, which it resembles on a large scale; hard lumps of ore and stone being crushed between two rollers in the same manner as coffee is ground by a hand-mill.

The mine, on being abandoned by Mr. Walton, was re-opened by a company, whose want of success testified the ripeness of their predecessor's judgment. It is remarkable, that one of the partners had discovered and applied for the vein only a *few hours* later than Mr. W., and now, after a lapse of many years, was doomed to possess only the shell from which so rich a kernel had been obtained. Such are the vicissitudes

M

of mining, ever liable to uncertainty. But in this, as in many other instances, it strikingly appears how much practical judgment and experience may be exercised in reducing that uncertainty to a great degree of probability.

A spirit of enterprise and increasing intelligence has made rapid progress during the present century. At the commencement of it, a Mineralogical Author * bears testimony that "the mines in Alston and Allendale are conducted on the most scientific principles, and the agents are men of skill and well versed in mechanics."

About this time the operations commenced which subsequently led to the discovery of Hudgill Burn Mine, the celebrity of which has given a new and powerful stimulus to mining adventure, and forms a prominent feature in the history and prosperity of Alston Moor. The following are some particulars relative to the discovery and productiveness of this important mine.

A trial for veins on the north side of the mountain of Middle Fell was commenced by the Flow-Edge Mining Company, who drove a level 250 fathoms in the tuft under the great limestone, and found only two weak veins. They sunk two shafts from the surface, and a *sump* or interior shaft to the four-fathom limestone, drove a flank level to the north, and made a rise to the middle flat of the great limestone in a vein which they discovered. This vein was explored for 20 fathoms, and produced a few trifling specimens of ore, but never any quantity worth washing and smelting. Such was the untoward result of four years mining adventure, and of an expenditure which may be estimated as follows :—

* Mawe, vide his " Mineralogy of Derbyshire."

250 Fathoms of Level, . . .	1250
Two Shafts, ...	175
Sump into Four-fathom Limestone, .	78
Flank Level, ...	100
Rise, and Drift in Vein, ; . .	62
Shop for Miners, Smithy, &c. . .	20
Wood Rails, ...	44
Waggons, Shaft Rollers, Kibbles, &c.	100
Agency, ...	100
	£ 1929

After thus losing nearly £ 2000, the company sold
the materials, abandoned the undertaking, and the
mine lay neglected for about eight years. In 1812,
Messrs. John and Jacob Wilson, with some other experienced miners, obtained leave to pursue the trial,
and accordingly having arched the entrance to the
level, cleared out the old workings, and laid new rails,
they continued the main level of the former company,
but altered its direction a little to the south. Four
men were employed to drive 20 fathoms of level in the
tuft, at four guineas per fathom, by which they made
16s. or 17s. per week. This partnership (two of whom
had shares and became wealthy proprietors of the
mine) continued working a year and three quarters;
the bargains being on an average about 3l. 10s. per
fathom, and in that time they drove about 70 fathoms
of level. In April, 1814, a vein was discovered which
had a good appearance, considering the stratum which
the level was then in, (the grey beds under the tuft),
but which would not in that situation pay for working.
After driving through the vein, which was 2 feet wide,
a rise was made to the low flat of the great limestone,
where the vein was nearly filled with carbonate of lead
or white ore. The partnership of four miners took a
bargain to work the vein at 18s. per bing until midsummer (9 weeks), and in that time raised 300 bings

of ore, and *cleared* £ 80 per man.   This was followed
by another bargain at 16*s.* per bing, by which the
same partnership cleared £ 25 each in three months.

Thus commenced, at wages of nearly £ 10 *per week,*
the working of those immense stores of wealth which
raised the proprietors to opulence, and have been a
source of extensive employment to the labouring classes
in Alston Moor.   The veins of Hudgill Burn have
since produced ore from 10 to 12 feet wide, and in
some places even as much as 20 feet.   The ease with
which it has generally been obtained is one great
cause of its value, being entirely worked by the pick
without the aid of blasting, at from 8*s.* to 10*s.* per bing.
For these wages the miner finds candles, conveys the
ore to the *day,* and pays for washing the ore, which
is very rich in quality.

The company spent about £ 360 before they reached
the vein, making altogether a sum of nearly £ 2300
expended in the discovery of this noble mine.   Of the
extent and value of Hudgill Burn Mine some idea
may be formed from the following circumstances:—
Its produce in 1820 was above 9000 bings of ore, in
1829 the horse levels exceeded four miles in length,
the value of silver produced in 1821 was £ 8400, and
the clear profit to the proprietors is supposed for many
years to have averaged about £ 30,000 per annum.

In 1812 the Commissioners of the Hospital agreed
to purchase the ore of those mining adventurers who
had no smelting establishment, and were without capital to abide the fluctuations of the market.   Mining
companies were thus alike sure of disposing of their
ore and receiving payment, an accommodation which
has had a highly beneficial effect in encouraging mining
speculation.

In 1817 a company took part of Langley Mills,

chiefly erected for their accommodation, for the purpose
of smelting the ores of zinc, which are found in abundance in some of the Alston veins.   These works were
successfully prosecuted for a few years; but the price
suddenly falling from £70 to £40 per ton, the concern
became a losing speculation, and was forthwith abandoned.   This metal is now furnished from Germany
at a less price than the English smelter can compete
with.

After this rapid sketch of the recent history of Alston
mining, it is proposed to give such a familiar description of the general nature and appearance of mines and
subterranean operations as may be intelligible to those
who have not had the opportunity of viewing them.

It has already been described that veins usually preserve a tolerably direct course, therefore the miner is often induced to follow the line of bearing, and to search for
the vein in some situation where it has yet been untried.
Sometimes a vein appears at the surface and especially
on the face of precipitous rocks, while mineral waters
and other external signs often indicate the presence
of mineral treasures.   The next point is to ascertain
whether a vein is likely to be productive, and in this
the experience of the practical miner is essential.
When a vein in Alston Moor is considered worthy of
trial, application is made to the agents for leave to try
the same, which is usually granted forthwith, (except
in extraordinary cases), for a specified period, commonly
of six months.   If, at the expiration of that time, the
trial is unsatisfactory, an extension of the term is
generally granted.   The parties making the trial are
bound to observe the following conditions:—To commence the trial within a month from the date of the
grant; the trial to be regularly continued till the end
of the term, and at least two pickmen daily employed

or an equivalent of labour; one-fifth part of any ore
raised to be paid as *duty* or rent to the Hospital, and
to observe all other conditions required in the leases
of lead-mines in this manor.   When a mine assumes a
promising and permanent aspect, a lease of the vein,
and, in some instances, a *general grant* of a parcel of
ground, including several veins, is obtained from the
Hospital.

In some particular situations the miner is compelled
to commence the trial of a vein by sinking a shaft,
but, owing to the hilly nature of the country, in nearly
every case a *level* or *adit* is driven from a hill side, and
in as favourable a stratum as the situation affords.
A *level* is a passage cut in the solid rock large enough
for the easy passage of men and horses, the usual dimensions being 3 feet wide at the bottom, gradually
widening to the middle height, where it is $3\frac{1}{2}$ or 4
feet wide, and from thence it has an arched form to
the top, which is from 6 to 7 feet high.   Levels are
most easily driven in plate beds, though they require
more support than in harder strata.   The cost of driving levels in different strata varies much according to
circumstances.   Even in plate beds the cost varies from
£1 to £6 per fathom, while hazel may cost £10 or
£12, and limestone still more.   A *horse level* seldom
departs from a very gentle and imperceptible rise, just
sufficient to allow the water to run along, and thus
a level begun in soft plate may by a rapid rise of strata
penetrate a hard stratum.   In some instances the
level is made to rise with the top of a hard stratum,
as at Nentforce High Level, which has a rapid ascent
to avoid penetrating the scar limestone.   On the floor
of levels, wood or iron rails are laid at the sides, which
greatly facilitate the passage of the waggons; the former convey sound to a great distance in the interior

of mines. Levels are driven either above or below the stratum intended to be worked, but, according to the improved practice of mining, if possible, *below*, in order that the work may fall down, and at one side of the vein, because the strata there are firmer than close to the vein.

From the level, access is had to the vein by a RISE, which is a shaft communicating from one side of the level to the vein. At the bottom there is usually a short level space left, 3 feet above the level sole or floor, for more conveniently putting the work into waggons. These rises are made at 15 or 20 fathoms distance from each other. But when it is necessary to descend either to the workings of a vein or for exploring lower strata, a shaft is sunk, sometimes walled, and sometimes formed irregularly in the rugged rock. This, which if commenced from the surface would have been called a shaft, is when underground denominated a *sump*.

When the vein is reached either by a rise or a sump, a *drift* is made about 6 feet high, and at least 2½ or 3 feet wide. The working of the vein is then prosecuted. If poor, the drift is continued in search of ore; if rich, the contents are regularly worked. This, and indeed nearly all mining work, is done by partnerships of four, six, or eight men, seldom of two, but sometimes, in very wet shafts or sumps, of twelve each. In driving levels or working veins, these partnerships have a certain length allotted them, generally 15 or 20 fathoms, and they either all work at different parts, or relieve each other alternately. The partnerships bargain with the master to work at a certain price for a specified period, and as these bargains are regulated by the present appearance and prospect of the strata or veins, a sudden and unexpected change may occur, productive either of gain or loss to the miner, as has been already instanced in the case of Hudgill Burn Mine. The bargain usually includes not only the labour in the mine, but also for gun-powder and candles, for the conveyance of the stone or ore, &c. to the *day* or outside of the mine, and also for washing and preparing it so as to be fit for smelting. It is by the bing of 8 cwt. of ore in this state, that the price of working is fixed. In some veins ore is easily obtained in a perfectly pure state; in others blasting with gun-powder is required. It generally happens that the ore is more or less mixed with veinstone, and sometimes the vein itself, however pure, is so thin, perhaps only 3 or 4 inches, that a great quantity of stone must be cut away for *drift room*, to allow space for working it. By all these circumstances the prices of mining labour are estimated, and it may easily be perceived how much it is the interest of the working miner to be well acquainted with the various appearances of strata and veins, that he may judge of and make his bargains accordingly. Hence a spirit of inquiry is created, which naturally extends to other subjects, and the miners generally possess a degree of shrewdness and intelligence rarely found in a labouring class of people.

Many of the rich veins of Hudgill Burn have been worked for 8s. or 10s. per bing; in Holyfield Mine at 14s. and 16s., while many veins cost from 34s. to 40s. and even a still greater sum; but the average in Alston Moor is generally estimated at rather above than under 30s. per bing. Four bings of ore are usually considered to produce a fother of lead; for this the mine owners raise 5 bings, one being paid as duty or rent to the Hospital. To this is to be added the cost of carriage to the smelt-mill, which, from the Alston mines, is usually to Langley, a distance of 13 miles, and costs 4s. or 5s. per bing. After this comes the charge for roasting and smelting, and for conveyance to the depôt at Newcastle, to constitute the cost of the production of lead. This cost is, however, to be doubled, or nearly so, to remunerate the mine owner for the original outlay incurred by the trial, and for the *dead work*, or that which produces no return, as driving levels, drifts, and other works. Mr. Taylor, one of the most experienced mining directors in England, states, that, judging of mining on a large scale, he is convinced that as much is paid for *dead work* as for raising ore.

After working a *length* in a productive vein, the excavation is filled up with *deads*, i. e. loose stones, rubbish, &c. from adjacent parts of the mine, * leaving only a *rise*, from which another *drift*, called a *heading*, is made, and the same operation is repeated to the top of the stratum, and above it if the vein continues productive. The rises are thus frequently 8 or 10 fathoms high, and have *stemples* or pieces of wood placed at two opposite sides, 4 or 5 feet above each other. These form a rude and apparently dangerous staircase, which the miner climbs with great ease and security, and down which the work is thrown from above to the *rise foot* below. Workings continued downwards under the first-made drift are called *stoups,* and in them the vein is worked downward from the bottom of the drift.

When a vein either continues productive or is expected to be so below the horse level, a sump is sunk to the required depth, which, if in soft strata, is walled, but in hard is left rugged and irregular. From the sump a drift is made, and the vein, if rich, is worked by headings and stoups as before,—the work being

* At Hudgill Burn Mine the workings have been so extensive that materials to fill them had to be brought from the *day.*

drawn up the sump by a hand whimsey, similar to what is used at draw-wells. In a flat vein the workings frequently run to a great extent, and the roof being supported by substantial posts of timber, the whole, especially when dimly lighted, presents a receding vista, which reminds the spectator of the aisles and pillars of a cathedral. When well lighted, the lowness of the roof destroys this effect, but the glittering treasures which adorn its sides are then presented to view, and are often exceedingly beautiful.

When the strata or veins are too hard for pick-work, recourse is had to blasting with gun-powder, which is done as follows. A round iron bar, called a *jumper*, having the end edged like a chisel, is held by one man while another strikes on the end until a hole is bored in the stone, usually 10 or 12 inches deep. A proper quantity of gun-powder is then placed in the hole, and a small iron rod or pricker is placed in it until plate or indurated clay is strongly pressed on the gun-powder, and the hole filled up. The pricker is then replaced by a paper squib tightly rolled up, and to this a slow match is applied, so as to leave time for the miners to retire to a safe distance, while the explosion effects in a single moment what long and laborious efforts would otherwise be required to accomplish.

The operation of blasting is sometimes one of almost inconceivable difficulty, and requires the most unwearying perseverance, combined with very arduous exertion. In most instances the result obtained is such as very amply to repay the labour, however great; for, by the exertion of a few hours added to a small quantity of gun-powder, large masses of hard rock are detached. Some of the borings in the copper ores of foreign countries seem comparatively to render the ordinary work of this kind in the English lead-mines a mere amusement. One account, extracted from a *proces verbal*, states, that in the Hartz Mountains, a workman was employed 88 hours in boring a hole 4 inches deep, during which time 201 boring augers were re-hardened, 26 remounted with steel, and 126 entirely destroyed. Instances of almost equal difficulty sometimes occur in the coal district, near Newcastle.

The ventilation of mines is now so much attended to, that choke damp or foul air is very rarely found in them. Among the improved methods of forcing pure air into lead-mines, the *water blast* is found to be one of the most efficient. The contrivance simply consists of a wooden pipe placed in a shaft, and down which a stream of water is kept running, while a quantity of fresh air is carried with it. From the bottom of this wooden pipe, another pipe of wood, iron, or lead is carried along the level, and the air being stopped by the water in a cistern at the bottom of the shaft pipe, and prevented rising by the downward current of air and water, is forced along the pipe into the workings of the mine. The water blast at Nentsbury engine shaft carries the air along a leaden pipe 600 yards, and at Scears Mine, in Teesdale, Mr. Stagg applied a hydraulic engine which ventilated a level a mile long, together with a rise of 65 fathoms. without any shafts being sunk from the surface. Other machines are in use for the same purpose, but to describe fully these various minutiæ would swell the subject to an unsuitable length.

Nearly all the waggons used in the lead-mines are made of strong oak, and run on metal wheels. Their dimensions are nearly as follows :—

	ft.	in.
Inside length at the top, ...	6	0
Ditto . . . . bottom, . . .	4	4
Ditto Breadth at the top, ...	1	6
Ditto . . . . bottom, . . .	0	10
Ditto Depth, ...	2	6
Height of the top of waggon from the ground,	4	0

At the bottom is a trap for letting out the contents, but some are made to *cant* or turn up like a common cart. Of late iron waggons have been tried in some mines, but they have not been much introduced in this manor. The partnership of miners pay the waggoners so much per *shift* of 8 waggon loads, according to the length of level, but the price is determined by proposals given in to the masters of the mine, whose interest it is to have the work done with the least expense to their workmen. The waggons are provided by the masters, but the horses are supplied by those to whom the *drawing of the work* is let. Sometimes a horse brings only one, but generally, on good metal rails, two waggon loads at a time, and will *draw* from 2 to 3 shifts (i. e. 16 to 24 waggons) in a day. The cost of drawing work usually varies from *3s.* to *8s* per shift, and no difference is made whether the contents be solid ore, or light earth and stone. The price includes the labour of filling the waggons in the mine, and afterwards depositing their contents either on the *bouse teams* or the *dead heap.*

All the work wrought in mines is included in the terms *ore, bouse,* and *deads.* The first of these has been already described. *Bouse* comprehends all the work that contains any portion of ore, and the term *deads* expressively denotes the stone, earth, and other substances excavated in the level or vein, &c. from which no profit is derived. The *bing stead, bouse team,* and *dead heap,* are the places where these different kinds of work are deposited at the outside of the mine.

In some places, where either the stratum or vein is hard, a partnership of six or eight men will scarcely work a shift of 8 waggons in a week, while in others two men can work that quantity, or even more, in a day. In a tolerably good vein a waggon will hold bouse containing a bing of ore, and in very rich veins two bings.

Early on a Monday morning, the streets of Alston ring with the clanking noise of heavy iron-shod clogs, and numerous groups of miners are seen departing to their subterranean labours, laden with jumpers, picks, &c.: many of them carrying an ample store of provisions for the week. They generally work eight hours a day, and 4, 5, or 6 days a week, according to circumstances. Some miners have small farms, which occupy their leisure time, while gardening and reading, these most delightful of all recreations, also form the leisure occupation of many.

Some of the mines are so near the residence of the workmen as to admit of their returning home between shifts, while others are situated amid wild and extensive hills and moors, far from any human habitation. Near the entrance of such remote mines is a house or mining shop with accommodation not only for the miners, but also for the smiths and joiners employed in making and repairing waggons, railways, &c. In the miners' apartment a number of beds are crowded in different parts; but it would be difficult by any description to convey an idea of the want of cleanliness and comfort which prevails in some of them. If Ledyard, who so beautifully and justly eulogized women for kindness and hospitality, had visited certain of these mining abodes, he would have praised them

N

with equal eloquence for the order and cleanliness
which we chiefly owe to their presiding care, and
which by the rougher sex are here so lamentably neglected.   To this description, however, there are some,
and it is to be hoped, increasing exceptions.   The
author recollects having seen in a mining shop on Crossfell, a set of very orderly regulations, and since then
has been much gratified by the clean and comfortable
arrangements of a large mining shop in Teesdale, lately
built under the direction of Mr. Stagg.   The discom-
forts of English mining, however, are few in comparison
with those of other countries.   The following account,
for instance, abridged from private letters of miners
who emigrated from Alston, gives a lamentable picture
of the Mexican miners.

" Their houses and clothing are of little value, the
former, for the most part, being miserable huts, which
it would be no hard task to erect in a single day.   In
families of seven or eight individuals, the furniture,
cooking utensils, in short, the whole contents of several
huts belonging to the labouring class which we examined, we never found to exceed twenty shillings in
value.   Not one house in twenty contained either knife,
fork, or spoon, and even in several whole villages they
could not be had.   As for beds, they never think of
such a thing, but lie down on the bare floor in a corner
of the hut.   The dress of the labouring man, when
new, would be thought dear for six shillings, and this
he wears at all times and in all places, in the mine and
out of it, on Sunday as well as ' *every day ;*' and at
night it serves both for bed and bed-clothes, until torn
off piece by piece."

If the Mexican miner falls short of English comforts and cleanliness, it appears that he much exceeds our miners in devotion; for the same intelligent

correspondent adds the following singular particulars : — " Sixty fathoms down the *Despache,* one of the entrances to Valenciana Mine, is a *church,* where lamps are continually lighted ; the workmen often spend half an hour in it on going to or retiring from work, and none of them pass without bowing before the painted images. They usually *spend an hour in singing* before they begin and the same after they leave off work."

VISIT TO A LEAD MINE.

Parties of ladies and gentlemen desirous of visiting the mines, can have suitable dresses provided by the landlord of the inn. A coat, pair of trowsers, and hat suffice for a gentleman, while the softer sex are often indebted to the landlady's wardrobe. Old shawls, hats, aprons, and even bedgowns, are taken to the mining shop, and the fair form of beauty and fashion is there disguised in such heterogeneous garments as to create no small share of amusement. The grotesque and novel appearance, both of ladies and gentlemen, frequently contributes not a little to the mirth of the company, and also tends to dissipate any timorous feeling. As mines, like states and empires, " have their periods of declension, and feel in their turn what distress and poverty are," it is thought better not to limit this sketch of a subterranean visit to any particular mine, but rather to describe such features as are generally presented in the Alston Mines. Permission to view the mines is in most instances readily obtained.

The author ventures from his own observation to premise, that visitors will generally be gratified with the rustic but kind civility and attention of the miners, and in some instances also with their intelligence, due allowance being made for local dialect and limited education. Their readiness to afford information and

to render assistance greatly contributes to the interest
and comfort of the excursion, by imparting knowledge
to the inquirer, and confidence to the timorous.

Arrived at the mine, the visitor has a full view of
the various apparatus used in washing the ore.   A lofty
heap of stones, clay, and other earthy substances, called
the dead heap, forms a prominent feature at the entrance
of all extensively wrought mines.   A railway carried
on a frame-work gallery over several deposits of *bouse*,
or mixed stone and ore, forms the *bouse teams*, and the
work of the separate partnerships of miners is divided
by partitions.   From these *bouse teams* the contents
are carried away to undergo the various and, it may
be said, amusing processes of washing; for strangers
who have leisure to examine them are usually much
entertained with the ingenious and cunning devices
to obtain every particle of ore.   In stone recesses,
called *bing steads*, sundry heaps of shining ore are laid,
some in broken lumps, and others in fine powder.
These are ready to be conveyed to the smelt-mills,
there to be converted into lead and silver, provided
the latter exists in sufficient proportion to repay the
expense of refining.

The party being suitably arrayed, have sometimes
to wait a little until the waggons come out, and in the
mean time are each furnished with a candle, round
which a piece of clay is fixed to hold it by.   At length
the rumbling noise of the approaching waggons rapidly
increases, and their contents having been deposited,
they are prepared for the visitors, the inside being
cleaned, and a board placed at each end for a seat.
The entrance to the mine, or *the level mouth*, resembles
an open arched door-way, into which the waggons are
driven at a moderate pace, and the visitors experience
the novel sensations which so unusual a conveyance is

apt to create.   The jolting, hottering motion of the
waggon, the splashing of the water, and the dark and
narrow passage, all concur to produce a strange effect,
which, however, soon wears off, and the subterranean
traveller finds leisure to observe the rugged roof and
walls of the level, or to listen to the guide urging forward his horse, in tones which the echoes of the mine
often render musical.   Even the fragment of a song
from the driver sometimes enlivens the journey, but,
on no account, is whistling allowed to be heard in
a mine.   The same prejudice exists among seamen,
but whence its origin is probably unknown.

After advancing some distance into the interior, the
visitor passes the rise foots, in some of which a store
of *bouse* is laid ready to be taken away, and at length
the waggons stop, and the company get out at one of
these openings.   A powerful vociferation of "*put
nought down*," is sent forth as a warning to those above
to throw no work down, and a further summons brings
a few miners to render their assistance.   When a signal
is to be made to some distance, it is done by beating
on the rails or posts, five beats, the first two slow, the
other three quick, and this is repeated several times.
The same signal is used in the Newcastle coal-mines,
where it is denominated "*jowling*."

The ascent of a rise is frequently attended with some
difficulty, especially to ladies ; but the gallantry of the
gentlemen and the effective civility of the miners soon
overcome the apparent dangers, and, one by one, they
are raised into the workings of the vein.   Hence the
party are conducted along the mine drift of the vein,
and this part of the expedition must of course greatly
vary in different mines; in all, however, the stranger
is apt to be impressed with feelings of awe at the idea
of being so far under-ground.   The contemplative

mind cannot but find many interesting subjects of reflection on the distribution of so much wealth in a
country otherwise so barren—the various uncertainties
which are the means of so extensive employment—the
fluctuations of fortune so often resulting from mining
adventures, and the ingenuity displayed in prosecuting
them, are all circumstances which may engage the
attention of a reflecting mind. To the mineralogist,
the interior of a mine, especially if it contain any spar-
encrusted caverns, is a sort of " home, sweet home,"
where the lovers of that science and of geology may
derive copious stores of intellectual enjoyment.

Blend and calamine, the ores of zinc, are sometimes
found spreading their glossy sparkling blackness in
the veins ; and fluor spar and quartz are the principal,
almost the only, sparry ornaments that abound. The
traveller at Alston is not gratified by the sight of such
beautiful caverns as are found in the Coalcleugh and
Allendale mines. The latter, however, being private
property, and worked by the proprietor, cannot be
considered as generally accessible to public curiosity,
though intelligent strangers of scientific pursuits will
doubtless receive every attention from the hospitality
and liberal-minded feeling of the resident agents.

The progress along vein workings is often " with
cautious steps and slow," especially among the intri-
cacies of flat workings. The friendly caution of " take
care ye dinna *fall* down the *rise,* sometimes calling the
visitor's attention (absorbed perhaps in other thoughts)
to a yawning gulf not to be passed over without some
caution. Sometimes an almost perfect stillness is
suddenly broken by a noise like distant thunder, the
report of a blast, which, rolling through the workings
of the mine, at length, after many reverberations, dies
away. The noise of work *" falling down a rise,"* and

the rumbling of waggons occasionally salute the ear;
the sound of the latter, gradually increasing and lessening, resembles the solemn effect of distant thunder.

The process of blasting has been already described.
The miners usually describe this and other modes of
working the ore, and frequently fire a *shot* for the
entertainment of the visitor; but, when near at hand,
the effect is by no means so striking as when distance
softens the noise and adds repeated echoes to it. At
length arrived at the far end or *forehead* of the vein, the
party usually rest, and a pleasant company is occasionally formed by the accession of two or three partnerships. Spirits or other refreshments are sometimes
taken by the visitors; and those who choose to spend
half an hour in the company of miners may frequently
derive both information and amusement. Most of the
miners are well acquainted with practical mining, and
with this is necessarily blended a knowledge of many
facts in geology and mineralogy. But many of them
are also tolerably well informed on other subjects, and
a friend of the author's was much surprised in one of
these forehead meetings, to hear Blackstone's Com-
mentaries quoted by a miner both with accuracy and
direct reference to the subject of discussion.

The miners work by what is often in other trades
called piece-work, so that the time spent with strangers
is taken from their own labour, and the prodigal expenditure of light is also at their own cost. By the
latter is meant the custom of miners of not putting
out their candles, however numerous the company may
be, and a forehead assemblage presents a brilliant illu-
mination, twenty or thirty candles being sometimes
placed against the wall. If any partners of the mine
are present, many are the speculations on the goodness and improving prospects of the *grove*. The

bonny dowk and *excellent rider,* as well as the ore, come
in for a share of gratulation, and are often considered
harbingers of the vein being still more productive.
Many a lively song and joke are often added to the
entertainment of such an assemblage as we are now
describing.   One example, spoken by a miner, may
suffice as a specimen of dialect and humour.   " An
folk wad nobbit let folk like folk as weel as folk wad
like to like folk, folk wad like folk as weel as folk ever
liked folk sin folk was folk !" It may here be remarked,
that the conversation of miners sometimes has a curious
effect from their assuming, as it were, a sort of volition
in the mineral world.   Thus they speak of a vein
being *frightened* to climb the hill, and that she therefore *swins away* to the sun side, (a feminine appella-
tion being generally used).   The throw of the strata
is attributed, as it were, to an *act* of the vein,—
" *she throws* the north cheek up."   These are homely
but they are also expressive modes of describing what
they have frequent occasion to speak of, and they
save a world of words.

Ladies seldom pursue a subterranean excursion further than the main workings, or such others as are
easily accessible, while their more adventurous companions frequently accompany the guides into other
parts of the mine.   In so doing, obstacles present
themselves more difficult of accomplishment than those
already described.   Lofty rises with rude and slippery
stemples * are sometimes found extremely awkward to
climb, and still more so to descend.   It sometimes
happens that the *stemples* are covered over with boards
to prevent their being injured by the falling ore, &c.
thrown from the workings above, and the only foot-

* See page 129.

holds then to be had are the spaces between these
boards.   The attention of the miners, however, who
climb and descend with perfect confidence, prevents
any real danger, though to a stranger the idea of
climbing fifty or a hundred feet on so perilous a footing
is seldom unattended with some sense of fearful ap-
prehension.

Journeying through the drifts of a narrow vein is a
less dangerous but often equally fatiguing task, especially if, by reason of accumulated work, the hands
and knees are to be put in requisition for several fathoms over sharp angular blocks of rock, which all but
fill the narrow passage.   At the end or forehead of
such drifts, buried as it were in a deep and lonely
cavern, a single miner is often found pursuing his
solitary labours at a string or thin vein of ore, which,
like a bright silvery stream, is seen traversing the rock.
It is considered that in general a solid rib of ore two
or three inches wide, will pay for working, and as a
much greater space is required for *vein room*, the pro-
curing of this slender thread of ore is attended with a
great proportion of unprofitable labour, hence the inconvenient but economical narrowness of the drift.   The
persevering visitor, who would explore every part of
a mine, after *descending the rise* to the level, is probably
next taken to a sump head, where he is required to
trust his person to a substantial rope hung on the axle
of a hand whimsey,* often of seemingly frail construction, and is thus lowered down into the deeper workings of the mine, the aspect of which is similar to
those above.

The subterranean researches of our visitors being at
length completed, the waggons are again entered, and

* A roller and handle similar to what are commonly used for
draw-wells.

the eye accustomed to such scenery surveys with greater clearness the strata of the roof and sides,—pendent drops are seen hanging from above, and the wooden posts, which in some places support the level roof, are covered with woolly snow-like fungi. The timorous sensations felt on entering are now dissipated, and the party can fearlessly look at these and other swiftly passing objects, on which at length a faint white gleam of light is seen to blend with the yellower rays of the candles. The rocky prominences become more and more illuminated, and the solar light, together with the sparkling drops of water impart so bright and silvery an aspect as to excite the greatest admiration. This rapidly increases until, amid the splashing of water and the noisy rattling of their rugged cars, the party emerge from the dark chambers of the earth to the magnificent and almost overpowering brightness of "THE DAY."

TEESDALE.

Yadmoss.—Cauldron Snout.—Tees Force.—Winch Bridge.—
Middleton in Teesdale.—Barnard Castle.

THE barrier between Alston Moor and the extensive
and romantic dale of the river Tees is formed by lofty
moors; the summit or "heaven's water division" of
which, and a mountain rivulet called Crookburn, form
the boundary between the counties of Cumberland
and Durham, and the parishes of Alston and Middleton
in Teesdale. That part of the moors which is crossed
by the new road, is called Yadmoss, a name which,
until lately, carried with it, to all who knew it, many
associations of a wild and barren country, of boisterous
weather, of bewildering mists, of snow storms, and of
the loss of human life. *

The almost impassable state of this dreary fell is
matter of historical record so far back as the reign of
Edward III. (see p. 8), and until a few years ago the

---

* One remarkable storm, about sixty years ago, was long
remembered by the name of the "Stoury Sunday." On this day
a young woman was lost in the snow on the adjoining moor.
A few weeks after, a person, going from Alston to visit his friends
in Yorkshire, was overtaken by a storm, and perished on Yadmoss. Other two persons were lost here about the same time.
The last person who lost his life in this unfortunate way was a
young man named Walton, who, visiting Middleton and returning the same day, missed his way on Yadmoss, and sunk exhausted
from the effects of storm and fatigue. The neighbouring fells
also have often been the scene of such calamities, and of still
more frequent personal hazard; for in such boisterous winds and
heavy falls of snow as often occur on these elevated moors, it was
almost impossible not to wander from the right path.

roads were of the most wretched description. But now on this as well as on the moors of Whitfield and Hartside, a good road has been constructed, guide posts have been erected, and the traveller may traverse the dreary heights of Yadmoss with ease and safety.

From Yadmoss the present road descends by the side of Harewood Beck, but will shortly be superseded by a new line, which, winding to the north, descends with a more gradual inclination, and then crossing the old road, passes near Tees Force, and joins the present road at Bowlees, near Newbiggin. From thence by Middleton and Barnard Castle to the Abbey Bridge at Rokeby, improvements on the present road, with occasional deviations, will complete an excellent line of road through the extensive district of Teesdale, and form an uninterrupted communication from Greta Bridge to either Brampton or Haydon Bridge by way of Alston.

In descending from Yadmoss, the tourist has, in clear weather, a commanding view of the vale of Tees. Around him are lofty round-topped fells, intersected by mountain streams, and in some few places discoloured by mine wastes. The lands in the middle distance have cottages scattered over numerous farms, consisting chiefly of pasture and meadow land, the bright green aspect of which imparts no unfavourable idea of the soil. These farms, and indeed the whole dale from thirty to forty miles in length, are the property of the Duke of Cleveland, and the tenancy is said to be scarcely less hereditary than the proprietorship, several farms having been transmitted from father to son for many generations. The houses are for the most part extremely rude in their construction, very picturesque withal, but somewhat too much in the style of Morland. Their being whitewashed partly redeems the poverty of their aspect, and this operation is said to be always performed, with becoming loyalty, on the approach of the most noble Duke to the moors in the shooting season.

The new roads will doubtless open the way to improvements in this interesting district, the capabilities of which are far superior to the condition which it is now in. At the present time, the dale head is so retired, and the ancient manners still so prevalent, that the tourist may find an interesting subject of speculation in the contrast which is thus afforded to a more crowded and artificial state of society. The clergyman of this secluded spot has resided here above thirty years, teaching a school during the week, and officiating twice in the Chapel every Sunday; establishments which are maintained by the Duke and Duchess of Cleveland. The general character of his humble flock would seem to indicate that he has been a useful labourer in this lonely vineyard.

A friend of the author's * has given the following graphic description of the scenery in High Teesdale.

" We pursued our way, sometimes scrambling over bold elevations, and at others plunging into deep and hidden recesses, until we reached the fell top, where we made a breathless pause. Here an extended prospect opened to our view. The romantic and varied scenery of Teesdale lay stretched out before us; the Tees seen in various points had a curious and picturesque appearance,—at one place it made a bold curve, at another a right angle, then was lost in a chasm, then sprang over a precipice, and then, as if tired of gamboling, swept proudly on in a straight line. The scenery was congenial to the stream; here a line of

* Mr. George Pearson, of Long Marton, in Westmorland.

terrific basaltic precipices carried the eye to the black and boundless wilds that stretched beyond,—there smiling woods, villages, white-washed hamlets, with the fugitive rivulets that were coming in from the mountains, mingled beautifully with each other, and formed a scene, that, to a poet's eye, might have been fraught with inspiration. How different was the view on our left. Nothing but a far-extended waste of heath was to be seen, bounded by a chaos of lowering and tremendous clouds, whose alpine ridges, catching the sunbeams at partial openings, produced a mimic representation of mountain scenery in all its fantastic and dismaying forms."

The farms in High Teesdale are chiefly occupied by miners, and however rustic the outside of their dwellings, the interior not unfrequently presents an admirable specimen of neatness, cleanliness, and order. The strength and activity of the hardy race of men who inhabit them are often equalled by kindness of disposition; and no one who has experienced their civilities can readily forget them, or attribute them to any other source than a well-meaning mind. As to women, as Ledyard says, they every where are kind and attentive. In this district they are remarkably so. If it be pleasing to contemplate excellence in works of fiction, it is still more refreshing and instructive to witness it in real life. A comely matron presiding in a humble but clean and neat abode,—the mother of blooming and athletic children,—a form and countenance retaining much of the grace and vivacity of youth,—a ready smile at once bespeaking a hospitable welcome and a cheerful mind,---manners free from awkwardness on the one hand, and from forwardness on the other, and apparently regulated by the influence of real kindness and genuine good sense. Such is a rapid sketch of female character, drawn in the lonely wilds of Teesdale, and the fidelity of the portrait was approved at the time by other and more competent judges than the artist.

The most interesting object that presents itself in a view of High Teesdale is the range of precipitous scars, which appear on the south side of the river. These columnar rocks, extending from behind the village of Holywick for several miles up the Tees, and forming a rugged promontory at Cronkley scars, are the basset of a range of basalt, which is inserted between the regular strata of the mountain limestone formation. Professor Sedgwick has devoted some time to the examination of this basalt or whin sill, and published, in the Cambridge Philosophical Transactions, an elaborate paper on the geology of High Teesdale. Besides being a most prominent and picturesque object in the general scenery of the dale, the whin sill is interesting to the tourist, inasmuch as it is the cause of, and the principal feature in, three of the most remarkable objects which, in High Teesdale, claim the traveller's attention. These are, Cauldron Snout, Tees Force, and Winch Bridge.

CAULDRON SNOUT.

Pedestrian tourists accustomed to mountain travelling may readily find their way from the descents of Yadmoss to this remarkable waterfall, but most visitors will do well to engage a guide, who may readily be procured by inquiry at any of the farms or "onsteads." From Harewood, access may nearly at all times be had on foot; but only in dry weather by horses. In either case it is a fatiguing journey of about three miles, chiefly over the steep and rugged sides of Harewood Fell. On gaining the summit of this lofty moor, an expansive but dreary prospect bursts upon the view. Wide and moss-covered moors extend in a gradual slope to the Tees, which here winds its way through a wilderness of the most stern and desolate aspect. In the distance a vast amphitheatre is formed by successive ranges of mountains in Yorkshire, Westmorland, and Cumberland, and which, towards the north, seem blended like waves into each other. But the bright spot and redeeming interest of this prospect is the Weel, whose waters, spread in the hollow of a vast and dreary basin, present a beautiful contrast to the dark heath of the barren moors which surround it, while its width and serpentine form give it the appearance of a broad river flowing through the midst of a desert.

The Weel is a sullen lake, in breadth about half a mile, and three or four times that length, formed by the interception of the Tees by basaltic rocks, over which the water flows into a deep and rapidly descending gorge, and forms the waterfall of Cauldron Snout.

On approaching the foot of the Weel, the rough road, over moss and ling, is suddenly more roughened by numerous projecting points and edges of basalt, which render either riding or walking both troublesome and somewhat dangerous. The author of an interesting little guide-book, the "Tour in Teesdale," gives the following testimony concerning the aspect of the adjacent scenery. "The conception of a scene so wild and magnificent, is difficult. Its extreme stillness and the desolate air of all you see are even oppressing. Not a house, a tree, nor inclosure of any kind interrupts the boundless waste;---not one dash of cheerful green animates the black and dreary heath; Chaos alone could be more terrific."

On descending the rocks at the foot of the Weel, the visitor beholds the waters of the Tees rushing with impetuous force down a steep basaltic chasm of two or three hundred yards in length. Near the top is a wooden bridge, thirty feet long, over the fall, from whence the visitor may view the swift and foaming current beneath. The fall is interesting at any time, even in very dry weather, the stream gamboling in its descent among the various channels which the rocks afford. But when the Tees is swoln with rains, it rushes down in one impetuous and unbroken torrent of almost resistless force, and, with its sides of frowning tower-like cliffs, forms a spectacle truly terrible and sublime.

Those who delight in the minor beauties of nature will here find them united with her boldest works. The variously-coloured lichen on the surface of the basalt is extremely beautiful, and not less so are the wild flowers which spring from the sides of the chasm. The examination of these, and viewing the fall from various situations, will, to most persons, afford much gratification. But it must be admitted that to some, and especially to ladies, the attractions of Cauldron Snout may scarcely repay the difficulties of the journey to it. A good horseman with a skilful guide may enjoy a ride on the rocky edges of scars, and over loose basaltic stone, deep moss-ruts, and frequent banks, both deep and stony; but it is well that the tourist should be apprised of this before he undertakes a jaunt in which such fatigues must necessarily be encountered.

Following the course of the Tees by rugged banks for nearly five miles, the tourist reaches the well-known cataract of High Force.

HIGH FORCE.

The river Tees, in traversing the mountainous country which has just been described, becomes rapidly augmented by various tributary streams, and, after its junction with Harewood Beck, assumes a wide and noble aspect. The fall of such a river, at fifteen miles from its source, over a precipice of upwards of fifty feet in height, may readily be conceived to be an object of the highest interest as regards remarkable and sublime scenery; and it is scarcely less interesting to the geologist from the clear developement of the strata it displays.

The river immediately above the fall is divided by a lofty rock into a greater and a less channel, the former of which in dry weather contains the whole stream, while at other times both channels are filled with impetuous torrents, which, rushing over the precipice, form a cataract on each side of the central mass of cliffs,---

"That rear their haughty head
"High o'er the river's darksome bed."

The principal channel is worn into a rugged descent at the edge, but the greater part, probably about 40 or 50 feet, is quite perpendicular, and over this the descent of so large a body of water at all times insures a gratifying treat to the lovers of natural scenery. The less channel is considerably worn, so that when dry a person may without much difficulty climb up it, and examine the junction of the basalt with the adjoining strata.

Hutchinson describes the main channel as having a perpendicular fall of 82 feet, but this is much over-rated. The height of the central rock is stated in the "Tour of Teesdale" to be only 63 feet, the entire perpendicular height of the fall probably does not exceed 50 feet, and the inclining falls above may be 15 or 20 feet more. Nearly one-half of the entire depth of the adjacent rocks consists of basalt, which, in the middle of the stream, towers up into a rugged but picturesque summit. Except in high floods, this station may easily be gained, and from thence the spectator can look down and behold the rolling tor-rent precipitated into the abyss below. Being on the giddy verge of so lofty a rock, the rapidity of the stream, the thundering noise with which it mingles with the deep sullen waters below, and the clouds of foam which often reflect the iris' lovely hues, alto-gether combine to produce mingled sensations of terror, astonishment, and delight.

Having taken this *inverted* view of the Force, the tourist, by walking about two hundred yards along the top of the banks on the north side of the river, will find a somewhat rugged but not very difficult descent down the rocks and underwood, and from the sides of the river may command a view of the falls at various distances. Here lofty precipices on each side form a magnificent amphitheatre, on the sides of which may be traced the rapid rise of the strata in a north-west direction, and the basalt regularly ranging with the other strata. The upper part and summit are more or less covered with brushwood and a few ash and yew trees, while, at the extremity of the vista, the ceaseless roar of the descending flood completes the majestic character of the scene.

WINCH BRIDGE.

A more slender, rickety, dangerous-looking structure than the old Winch Bridge, it would be difficult to conceive, and the stranger possessed some courage who ventured across, although the neighbouring inhabitants were in the habit of passing along it, to the number of fifty or sixty daily. It has been lately replaced; and though the present structure possesses not the claims of its predecessor either to antiquity or *craziness*, yet the situation and romantic scenery of the river and its basaltic rocks on each side may well repay so short a walk as a quarter of a mile from the turnpike road at Bowlees House.

The old bridge is said to have been the earliest suspension bridge in Europe; but the claim to this distinction must of necessity be very uncertain, as similar structures may have existed in mountainous and secluded situations at an earlier period. The author learnt from respectable authority in Teesdale, that Winch Bridge was known to have been built upwards of eighty years ago, and though the wood-

work has been frequently replaced, the nearly worn-
out chains bore testimony of long decay.

The dimensions of this singular structure, and its
height from the surface of the river, have been greatly
exaggerated in most descriptions. Thus Hutchinson
calls the chasm 60 feet in depth, and the bridge 70
feet long. The " Tour in Teesdale" gives the depth 50
feet, and the length 63 feet. The correct dimensions
are as follows :---*

	ft.	in.
Length of bridge between the rocks,	59	4
Length of chain supported by the rock on the north side,	12	0
Length of ditto on the south side not visible, being covered with earth,		
Centre of bridge lower than the ends, about	3	0
Height of bridge above the surface,	21	0
Depth of the river,	8	6

The links were about 6 in. long and 1¾ in. broad,
and the iron bar of which they were formed was ½ in.
and ⅜ in. thick. These chains were fixed by bolts
into the rock at each end, and on them were laid
wooden cross-rails 3½ feet distant; on these were laid
deals lengthwise, forming a floor 1 ft. 9 in. broad,
with a hand-rail 2 ft. 9 in. high on each side. Less
chains were placed near the ends, and fixed to the
rocks at a little distance to prevent the swinging, but
most imperfectly was their office performed.

Let the reader then imagine so flimsy a fabric in so
ruinous a state; the chains decaying, the floor in some
parts open, in others rotten, and the broken hand-rail

* See " Description of Winch Bridge, the oldest suspension
bridge in England; by W. C. Trevelyan, Esq." In Brewster's
Philosophical Journal, 1828. Some of the iron links, almost
worn through, are preserved in the Museum at Wallington.

on each side yielding as soon as touched; to these let him add the unearthly creaking and the trembling instability of the whole, bending at every step, and he may form some idea of a structure which far more resembled a trap for human life than a regular communication between two counties.

In August 1820, one of the chains gave way while eleven persons were passing over, most of whom were on it at the same time. Two of them fell into the river and were saved; but one, falling on the rocks, perished. The bridge was soon after repaired by the late Earl of Strathmore, and is now entirely replaced by a more substantial fabric.

The village of Holwick and its adjoining scenery are worthy of the tourist's attention. He will there find the whin sill in that prominent station which it occupies in all the most interesting scenery of High Teesdale.

Having in these descriptions diverged considerably from the main road, the following distances may be useful :---

			Present Road.	*New Road.*
From Alston to	Eshgill Burn,	.	5 miles.	5 miles.
. . .	Crookburn, .	.	8½ do.	8½ do.
. . .	Langdown Beck,		14 do.	14¼ do.
. . .	Bowlees, .	.	18 do.	18½ do.
. . .	Middleton, .	.	21 do.	21½ do.

The land about High Force and Winch Bridge presents a kind of intermediate scenery between the barren mountain and the richly cultivated vale. Stone walls and rustic hamlets are superseded by hedges and comfortable farm-houses, while that most beautiful of all nature's ornaments, the tree, begins to enrich the aspect of the country, and the eye looks forward to increasing fertility and beauty. After passing the village of Newbiggin, the tourist proceeds by a pleasant ride of $2\frac{1}{2}$ miles to

MIDDLETON IN TEESDALE.

Contrasts have great influence in our judgment of comparative objects, and this is strikingly exemplified in the different effects produced by ascending and by descending an extensive dale. A tourist from the rugged heights of Yadmoss, and another from the luxuriant scenery down the vale, form very different ideas of the situation of Middleton. The former, pleased with the approaching signs of cultivation, will probably admire the adjacent scenery; while the latter, with the author of the " Tour in Teesdale," may consider it " in the midst of a wild and uncultivated region."

Middleton, usually called MIDDLETON IN TEESDALE, to distinguish it from another place of the same name near Darlington, may be considered the capital of High Teesdale, and is a market town, containing about 1820 inhabitants, of whom the greater number are employed in the neighbouring mines. The scenery in the immediate vicinity of the town is extremely pleasant, and the moss-clad moors impart to it a romantic aspect. On the left, on entering the town, is the handsome residence of Robert Stagg, Esq., agent to the London Lead-Company, who has greatly improved the adjoining ground, and transformed an uneven boggy waste into smooth and beautiful lawns. The houses of the town are spread over a considerable extent, and the river and trees being often seen through the various openings, give it a lively and pleasant appearance. The church is a plain and very ancient structure, and the living is a rectory in the gift of the king. The river Tees is here crossed by a handsome bridge of one arch, of 80 feet span, built about 20 years ago on the ruins of a former *new* bridge, which, in the winter of 1811, fell when nearly completed.

The tourist will be much gratified by an inspection of what may be called the new town of Middleton. This consists of a number of extremely neat and comfortable dwelling-houses built in several uniform rows in a spacious garden, entered by a handsome stone arch; each cottage has its respective portion of garden ground. The whole is the work of the London Lead-Company, executed from the chaste and appropriate designs of Mr. Bonomi, under the direction of their active and highly intelligent manager, Mr. Stagg, whose exertions to promote at once the interests of the company, and the comforts of the miner, cannot be too highly commended.

A national school has been erected, and is chiefly supported by the Lead Company, whose workmen obtain the advantages of education at a very moderate rate. A library is also attached to it for the use of the miners.

Forster, in his Section of the Strata, enumerates 38 mines in Teesdale; and, with a few exceptions, the whole of the mineral district is now in the occupation of the London Lead-Company. The mines at Manor Gill and Lodge Syke, near Middleton, have been immensely rich, and both the subterranean workings and the machinery at the washing-floors well deserve the attention of the curious, " who may," says the author of the ' Tour in Teesdale,' " by proper application be allowed to visit the interior." It is obvious, however, that the mining concerns of individuals or private companies cannot be considered accessible to mere public curiosity, the frequent intrusion of which would be extremely inconvenient. Intelligence and science

P

may doubtless be assured of due attention to their
objects; but it may be observed, that the general
regulations of the company indicate a wish to avoid
notoriety or much interruption to the usual routine of
their works.

It would greatly exceed our limits to enter into a
minute description of every remarkable feature or
interesting prospect which merits attention.   The
tourist who spends a few days of fine weather at
Middleton, and can leisurely examine the country
from thence to Barnard-Castle, may rest assured of
enjoying many a rare example of the charms

> "Which Nature to her votary yields."

The road on the Yorkshire side abounds in rich
woody scenery and pleasant villages; that on the
other side passes over high lands, and commands more
extensive and distant prospects.   In the former route
the tourist passes through the villages of Mickleton,
Romaldkirk, Cotherstone, and Lartington.   In these
many neat and comfortable and some very handsome
houses, shaded by "tall ancestral trees," bring to mind
Mrs. Hemans' beautiful little poem — "The Homes of
England."   Nor can we view the cheerful home, the
stately trees, and the lively village green, without
feeling a cordial and enthusiastic sympathy with the
concluding apostrophe : —

> "And green for ever be the ground,
> "And bright the flowery sod,
> "Where first the child's glad spirit loves
> "Its country and its God!"

During summer and autumn, Lartington is extremely beautiful from the abundant foliage in and
near it.   The Hall is a handsome residence, with a
spacious lawn in front, and, as well as the neighbouring estate, is the property of H. Witham, Esq.   From

thence is a short and pleasant ride or walk to Barnard-Castle. On the north side the scenery at Egglestone claims attention. The Hall (the seat of G. Hutchinson, Esq.) is surrounded by beautiful pleasure-grounds, comprising a lofty waterfall and subterranean walk, and the church stands in the middle of what was laid out by the late Mr. Hutchinson as a botanical garden.

Egglestone smelt-mill, the property of the London Lead-Company, was erected a few years ago, under the immediate direction of Mr. Stagg, and is undoubtedly the most complete establishment of the kind in the north of England. The author, with Mr. Stagg's permission, had the satisfaction of seeing the whole interior; and no one in viewing it can fail to be much gratified with the regularity and economy of labour with which the various processes are conducted. The situation is so chosen, and the building so constructed, that the *ore* may require no lifting, but *descend* from process to process until it is brought out as *lead* at the lower part of the mill.

The high lands over which the road passes to Barnard-Castle command prospects both up and down the Tees, which the eye may rest on for some time with great pleasure, but which the mind can form a very faint idea of from any delineations either of the pen or the pencil. Suffice it to say, that on the one hand is seen an extensive view of High Teesdale, bounded by lofty hills, covered by the summit of Cross-Fell; and on the other the umbrageous and fertile lands through which the Tees pursues its way to the German Ocean.

BARNARD-CASTLE.

The august and venerable walls of a once-powerful fortress attract the attention of the tourist, who, for the first time, approaches this ancient and interesting town. Nor is the beauty of the adjacent scenery less calculated to excite his admiration, presenting, as it does, a variety of inimitable prospects, which, to every lover of nature, afford the promise of rich enjoyment. A picturesque bridge, which, in conjunction with the castle ruins, has often been the subject of the artist's skill, forms the south entrance into the town. The two pointed and ribbed arches of this bridge are of unequal size, and their ancient aspect, so much in unison with the adjacent rocks and ruins, present a striking contrast to the more formal structures of the present day.

The principal road through the town continues northward by a wide and well-built street, which steeply ascends to a large octangular building, the basement of which is formed by a piazza of plain Tuscan columns, inclosing a market-place for the sale of poultry, &c. Within this is a common prison, and above it are spacious rooms for the magistracy. It was erected in 1747. While its uniform appearance certainly constitutes it an ornament of the town, its situation in the middle of a public thoroughfare, like the corresponding buildings at Berwick upon Tweed and Stockton, in some measure interferes both with the convenience and the beauty of the street. From the town-hall a pleasant street leads past the church, a venerable structure dedicated to St. Mary. Some of the windows merit the attention of those who admire English, or, as it is more commonly called, Gothic architecture. Against the outside of the wall, at the east end of the chancel, is a curious monumental stone, a wood cut of which is inserted in Surtees' History of Durham, together with a beautiful engraving of the church. The building is in good preservation, and the interior no longer deserves the severe animadversion which the spirited pen of Hutchinson so liberally bestowed upon it. "The inside of the church," he observes, " is wretchedly stalled, the pavement broken and uneven, and the whole appearance slovenly and offensive." New pews erected in 1813, the addition of a fine-toned organ in 1823, and other additions and repairs, have restored this once ruinous interior to a respectable and venerable aspect. The tower is 60 feet high, contains 8 bells, and had formerly a leaden spire, which was removed 40 years ago. The living is a curacy, in the patronage of the Vicar of Gainford, of which parish Barnard-Castle is a chapelry.

At the corner of the street leading from the townhall eastward is a curious and seemingly very ancient stone about 4 feet high, on which, in bold but ruinous relief, is an apparently ecclesiastical figure. His features have yielded to the silent ravages of time, aided not a little perhaps by the rude attacks of boyish thoughtlessness ; and, in more legible preservation, —

" A beard descending sweeps his aged breast."

On each side is a boar rampant, which appear on the most friendly terms with their venerable companion. These singular figures probably represent some monkish legend.

Near the town-house are the two principal inns and posting-houses, the King's Head and the Rose and Crown, where the traveller may depend on enjoying all the accustomed ease and comforts of " mine inn;" and northward from thence the street is very wide, and contains many large and well-built houses with excellent shops. These, with the surprising bustle and activity of the weekly market (held on Wednesdays) are strongly characteristic of what Barnard-Castle really is, the metropolis of a large portion of the vale of Tees and an extensive range of the adjacent mountainous region.

The ruins of the castle occupy a space of nearly seven acres, lying between the market-place and the river. The usual access to them is by a short lane between the inns referred to above, which leads to the ruins of one of the castle gates. This opens to a spacious green, bordered towards the south end by small gardens and the imperfect ruins of part of the castle walls, while in front and towards the north-west appear more extensive and important remains. Interesting from their antiquity and history, these walls, now so desolated, present few details of architectural interest. This part of the castle area is separated from the green by a fosse, and is thrown into gardens, occupied by different individuals. Into one of these gardens the western port or gate of the castle opens, and in another is a fine window, evidently of much later date than the castle, and which has also been improved by modern repair. This window, of what some would style Elizabethian architecture, is commonly called the Boar Window, from the insignia of a boar inserted in the upper part of it.

The eye may tire with beholding dark and gloomy walls, and the mind may be saddened by the melancholy reflections which are apt to arise amid the desolation of once royal halls. For the soul of music and the revelry of stately feasts have for ever departed, and the once proud fortress, which frowned defiance from its rock-built basis, now resembles an aged and withering oak, trembling on a precipice, and seeming ever ready to fall; but, though many a branch is riven, and though its trunk is reft by the lightning's arm of fire, yet still it stands, and future generations may behold the scarcely lessened vestige of its ruins.

But at the Boar Window neither the eye nor the mind need long be oppressed; for a small square window on the left affords a speedy relief. On entering the rustic door of this opening, a beautiful and extensive prospect bursts on the view. One wide and fair feature of it has been drawn with pictorial truth. A stately stream spread before the eye, and receding in beautiful perspective in the midst of rocky and woody banks, unfolds to the delighted eye

> " Where Tees, full many a fathom low,
> " Wears with his rage no common foe,
> " For pebbly bank nor sand-bed here,
> " Nor clay-mound checks his fierce career;
> " Condemned to mine a channel'd way
> " O'er hardest sheets of marbled grey."

Of the surrounding landscape it may be sufficient to add, that, owing to the height of the rock on which the castle stands, the prospect is extensive; that the surface is diversified by several rounded hills, abounding either in masses or belts of wood, while the fields to a considerable distance have hedge-row trees, which impart great beauty. The distance unfolds the blue moors of the west, and the fore-ground the rocky steeps of the castle base, with waving trees and the broad and noble stream of Tees. Such are the rough and imperfect outlines of a scene which the pencil of Turner or Swinburne * would inimitably pourtray.

---

* The powerful charms of Turner's landscape are well known through the medium of the London exhibitions and of many splendidly engraved works. The drawings of Edward Swinburne, Esq., senr. (brother to Sir J. E. Swinburne, Bart. of Capheaton) are inimitably beautiful, and exhibit the finished and delicate touch of an experienced and accomplished artist.

A wide footpath from the bridge climbs by a gradual ascent the abrupt and precipitous steeps on which the castle stands, and, extending past the western gate of the castle, communicates with the town.   Midway on this picturesque walk, the spectator looks up and beholds with terror the upright walls of a lofty tower standing on the very brink of the precipice.   From this footpath several others descend to the narrow holmes adjoining the river, and from thence the castle is seen to great advantage.   A large round tower on the left is called Brackenbury's Tower, and from it the walls and towers extending along the rock, tinted with the venerable hue of age and partially covered with ivy, with the ancient bridge, a prominent object in the distance, form a scene at once interesting to the antiquary and to the admirer of fine scenery.   This view is very beautifully delineated in an exquisite engraving in Surtees' splendid History of Durham, in which also the scenery of the Tees is illustrated by engravings from drawings by Edward Swinburne, Esq.

At Barnard-Castle the tourist has fairly emerged from the barren wildness of the mining districts, and entered on a fair and fertile region.   Here, for the first time, the route down the vale of Tees is intersected by public conveyances, and this accommodation renders Barnard-Castle a suitable place for the commencement or the termination of a mining tour in Teesdale.

It would far exceed the limit of these pages to offer any description of the numerous and attractive objects of attention which abound in this interesting district. The romantic woods at Rokeby have attained a wide celebrity, and who ever viewed the secluded grandeur of its scenery without the liveliest feelings of pleasure. Rock piled upon rock, and trees rising above trees to a stupendous height, with smooth green lawns and the murmuring waters of the Greta tinged with the brown hue of the mossy hills. The ivy tendrils hanging in midway air, and the tall grey cliffs crowned with majestic foliage. The grey ruins of Egglestone, and, in short, the whole of this vicinity is sacred ground to the worshiper of Nature. The pens of Scott and Surtees, and the pencils of Turner and Swinburne, have been employed, with an excellence far beyond encomium, in illustrating the splendid attractions and interesting history of Teesdale, and

Well may my feeble pencil shun
A task which master hands so well have done.

WEARDALE.

Durham. — Cathedral. — Bishop-Auckland. — Stanhope. — Head
of Weardale.

———

HAVING ended the descriptive notices of Teesdale at
Barnard-Castle as the highest place in the valley which
affords public conveyance to the traveller, the city of
Durham claims a similar notice, for no coaches traverse
the valley of Weardale west of this ancient and picturesque seat of episcopacy. There are not perhaps in all
England three contiguous dales of greater interest and
beauty than the mining dales of Tyne, Wear, and Tees,
and yet they are comparatively unknown to the public.
Our venerable and respected townsman, WILLIAM
TURNER, (a name which will be long perpetuated
by all who duly regard the union of moral worth with
the constant and useful exertion of superior talents),
in a paper written forty years ago thus justly comments
on the scenery of these fine rivers. "The views down
the Wear from the hill above Wolsingham were sufficient to excite an ardent curiosity to trace that beautiful
river from this place to its junction with the sea.
Indeed, so great are the beauties of this fine stream,
which so delightfully meanders through this palatinate,
while its sister streams, rising from the same point and
separating themselves at nearly equal distances, mark
for the most part the boundaries of the county to the
north and south, that I am persuaded a painter of
taste would here find ample employment for his pencil;
and that the encouragement of the public would render
it not only a pleasing but a lucrative task to sketch

out the picturesque beauties of the rivers Tyne, Wear, and Tees."

The object of the present volume is not to offer a detailed description of the extensive districts included within the compass of these vales, but by brief sketches to convey a feeling of scenery and other attractions which are little known, but which so eminently deserve more general notice and admiration. Several works already before the public afford minute details of the history and topography of Weardale. The following are, therefore, merely brief memoirs of such subjects and places as seemed most interesting to the author in a pedestrian tour from the city of Durham to the head of Weardale, together with extracts relative to the principal objects which claim the tourist's attention.

Durham has been called "The Zion of England." He that hath eyes to see, and ears to hear, may, from the scenery of its banks and the music of its cathedral, derive the highest pleasures that these inestimable gifts enable us to enjoy. The contemplative traveller will need little recommendation to

> " Spend some lone and pleasant hours
> By Durham's stately woods and towers,
> And with delighted gaze admire
> Each castled steep and lofty spire,
> Where on each time-worn wall is told
> A tale of ages venerably old.
>
> Mean time the Abbey's tinkling bell,
> Like some monastic chapel's knell,
> Tolls through the woods, and bids repair
> To choral songs and chanted prayer,
> Where the loud organ's sweet-ton'd chord
> Accompanies the sacred word,
> Till the vast temple all rebounds
> With solemn and majestic sounds,
> That roll in stately thunders through
> Each long-drawn aisle and vaulted avenue."

The architectural composition of the eastern portion or choir, and chapel of the Nine Altars in Durham Cathedral is uncommonly grand.   The marble floor,— the beautifully-carved stalls, surmounted with splendid tabernacled spires,—the elevated throne of the prelate, and rich adornments of Bishop Hatfield's monument,— the light and elegant screen of the chancel,—the lofty marble pillars and richly-clustered foliage on the walls,---the massive and deeply-cut Norman pillars,--- the lofty roof and magnificent wheel window of the Nine Altars present a spectacle of awful, venerable grandeur, that stamps a deep impressive feeling on every contemplative mind.

And these attractions, powerful as they are, are increased by the effect of Divine Service as daily performed here.---Vibrated with the chords of the noble organ, accompanied by the sweet music of the choir,--- the tender cadence---the deep pathos and mournful sublimity of the chanted responses, the ear is filled with perfect music, which leaves a delightful remembrance on which the mind dwells with pleasure;---so exquisitely perfect is the Choir of Durham Cathedral in this department of the musical service.

Durham Castle is more curious than beautiful.   The interior, particularly the north front, is uncommonly picturesque, but the interior is far exceeded in beauty by many places of much less importance.   The entrance hall is a large and lofty room, paneled with oak, adorned with paintings of the Apostles, and a good one of Charles I.   From this the visitor enters a room with a dark oak floor, in which is a large Italian painting " Cupid in a forest," also some curious representations of the Great Church of Milan and other structures.   The Bishop's Gallery is a long plain apartment, adorned with numerous engravings of

Cathedrals. At one end is a small private Chapel, with some curious wood carving. From this gallery a door-way was opened out a few years ago by the discovery of a fine Norman arch adorned with splendid architectural enrichments; an engraving of which forms one of the elegant illustrations to Surtees' Durham. Some of the rooms are hung with tapestry of great age, and the mansion contains many objects well deserving the attention of the tourist.

From Durham, the traveller who intends to explore the beauties of Weardale will make Bishop-Auckland his first place of destination, and, accordingly as time and mode of travelling admit, may devote more or less attention to the several objects which claim inspection. The views in the neighbourhood of Durham will prove highly interesting from the beautiful combinations of the Castle and Cathedral with the rich foliage of the adjacent banks. About a mile west of the city are the remains of Neville's Cross, on the side of the turn-pike road. Of this once lofty and ornamented cross little remains except the steps which formed its base. May its hastening to oblivion be emblematical of the forgotten horrors of war, from which this isle has so long been preserved, and the angry spirit of which seems yielding to that influence of time which effects so many changes. The cross was erected by Ralph Lord Neville, in commemoration of a battle fought at this spot between the English and Scottish armies, on October 17th, 1346. Davies, in his "Rights and Monuments," thus describes it when perfect.

"On the west side of the city of Durham, where two roads pass each other, a most famous and elegant cross of stone-work was erected to the honour of God, for the victory there obtained, known by the name of Nevill's Cross, and built at the sole cost of Lord Ralph

Q

Nevill; which cross had seven steps about it, every way squared to the socket wherein the stalk of the cross stood, which socket was fastened to a large square stone; the sole or bottom stone being of a great thickness, viz. a yard and a half every way: This stone was the eighth step. The stalk of the cross was in length three yards and a half up to the boss, having eight sides all of one piece; from the socket it was fixed into the boss above, into which boss the stalk was deeply soldered with lead. In the midst of the stalk in every second square, was the Nevill's Cross; a saltire in a scutcheon being Lord Nevill's arms, finely cut; and at every corner of the socket was a picture of one of the four Evangelists, finely set forth and carved. The boss at the top of the stalk was an octangular stone, finely cut and bordered, and most curiously wrought; and in every square of the nether side, was Nevill's Cross in one square, and the bull's head in the next, so in the same reciprocal order about the boss. On the top of the boss was a stalk of stone, (being a cross a little higher than the rest) whereon was cut, on both sides of the stalk, the picture of our Saviour Christ, crucified; the picture of the Blessed Virgin on one side, and St. John the Evangelist on the other; both standing on the top of the boss. All which pictures were most artificially wrought together, and finely carved out of the entire stone; some parts thereof thorough carved work, both on the east and west sides of the cross, with a cover of stone likewise over their heads, being all most finely and curiously wrought together out of the same hollow stone; which cover had a covering of lead. It remained till the year 1589, when the same was broken down and defaced by some lewd and wicked persons."

From Neville's Cross a pleasant road leads to the

village of Brancepeth, where a venerable Church and
stately Castle deserve the tourist's attention.   The
following account of this fine baronial mansion is
extracted from a local guide-book. *

Brancepeth Castle, the magnificent residence of
William Russell, Esq., was originally erected by the
Bulmers, a family of great antiquity, and who were
seated here for many generations.   The castle of
Brancepeth has been strongly fortified, and defended
by a cantonment of towers.   Leland in his Itin. vol.
1. p. 62. 71, &c. says — " Strongly set and buildid,
and hath 2 courtes of high building. — There is a little
mote that hemmith a great piece of the first court. — In
this court be 3 towers of logging, and three smaule
adornaments.---The pleasure of the castelle is in the 2
court, and entering into it by a great toure, I saw in
schochin, in the fronte of it a lion rampaunt.   On the
southe west part of the castelle cummith doune a little
bek out o' the rokkes and hilles not far of.   Sum say
that Rafe Nevile, the first Erle of Westmerland, buildid
much of this house, A. D. 1398.   The Erle that now
is hath set a new peace of work to it."

Hutchinson, describing the castle as it was in his
day, and prior to the late alteration, says, " Within
the works is a spacious area, which you enter from
the north by a gate with a portcullis, and defended
by two square towers.   The area is of no regular
figure, and the works which surround it, though very
strong, have no distinguishing marks, by which a
conjecture can be formed as to their age.   The parts
now inhabited lie on the south-west side of the area,
and appear to have been connected by works of various
ages ; the original plan in that part seems to have

* Historical and Descriptive View of the City of Durham.

consisted of four distinct square towers, whose angles
project as buttresses, with a small turret at the top of
each angle, hanging on corbles, open at the sides, and
not in front. From the gate, on the east side, is a
long stretch of wall, with a parapet, which communicates with a large square tower, having projecting
angles, turreted like those described; from this tower
the wall communicates, at no great distance, with
another large tower similar to the last, and thence the
wall stretches to the inhabited part of the castle,
broken only by a small turret, square in front, but
octagonal towards the court. From the gate on the
west is a high wall, the parapet in many parts hangs
on corbles; where the wall forms angles, it is gar-
nished with small square turrets, on the area side
supported by an arch; and in the floor of each is a
square aperture to receive materials from persons
below, whereby the guard should annoy those who
assailed the wall. Towards the north and east the
castle has been defended by a moat; to the south and
west the walls rise from a rock, nearly forty feet
in height, watered by a small brook. The hills to the
west are lofty. It is probable the whole fortress consisted originally of a race or series of towers, of similar
form; for the west wall and angular turrets are much
more modern than the fortifications on the east. If
this conjecture is allowed, then the fortress would
contain a cantonment of eight large towers, exclusive
of those defending the gateway. One matter, which
seems necessary to observe, points out the great antiquity of this castle, that our records furnish us with
no licence for fortifying and embattling; which is not
the case of any other in the county, except Barnard-
Castle: And so early as the 27th year of Bishop

Hatfield, it is styled in the records, the barony of Brancepeth."

The old castle, with the surrounding wall, was almost entirely pulled down, and a new one was begun during the life of the present possessor's highly respected and much-lamented father, the late Matthew Russell, Esq., M. P., which, from all appearance, is likely to equal in magnificence and grandeur, any of the noble residences in the north of England. That portion of the old castle, which was suffered to remain entire, has been fitted up to afford a present residence to the family. In this part, the apartments are of a very noble description; amongst them is the *Baron's Hall*, lighted at the sides by stained glass windows, and at the west end by a richly-painted window, in three beautiful compartments, representing three distinct views of the memorable battle of Neville's Cross, fought between the English and Scotch, in 1346. These windows were erected in 1821, by Mr. Collins, of London. Considerable alterations have been made, and are likely to take place, in the disposition of the gardens, pleasure grounds, &c. The park is well stocked with fine deer, and has been lately enlarged by the addition of upwards of 100 acres of land.

From Brancepeth tolerably good roads, shaded with lofty hedges and numerous trees, lead through the village of Willington, and from thence ascend an eminence called Rumby Hill; and here the prospect, which all the way from Durham has been exceedingly fine, becomes more expanded; the eye ranges with delight over an extensive survey of well-cultivated and wooded ground. Croxdale Abbey is a fine object from many parts of the road. Its plantations form an agreeable contrast to the long and thickly-intersecting lines of hedges and hedge-row trees, which give the adjacent hills an appearance of cultivation exceeding the quality of the land, which, however, near to the river is very good. But the higher portions, though much inferior, seem, on a distant view, very fertile from the wood so plentifully stretched along the inclosures of the gently-sloping sides of the vale.

On reaching the summit of Rumby Hill at a toll-house, there opens suddenly to view a new and unexpected prospect, formed by a hollow or basin, with slopes apparently descending on every side, and presenting the same wooded and varied features which appear in the distant prospect.

Bishop-Auckland stretches along a commanding eminence, and is surrounded with rich and lovely scenery. The western extremity consists of mean cottages, occupied by a numerous vagrant tribe, who, from this centre of seldom-inhabited homes, issue forth to vend their brooms, mugs, and other commodities.

From hence a spacious street extends eastward, and branches into two or three smaller streets, continuing in the same direction, which terminate in a handsome square. Here is a chapel of ease, with a tower and decorated pinnacles, and a school, a neat stone building, erected by that munificent patron of good works, the venerable Barrington, of whom the remembrance appears to be gratefully cherished by the neighbouring inhabitants.

From this square or market-place, an avenue, formed by very respectable houses, continues east-ward to the gateway or entrance to the Bishop's Park, which exhibits a variety of rich scenery. The Bishop's Palace is finely situated on an eminence. The exterior is plain, and its appearance derives great beauty from a stone screen with open pointed arches at a little distance from the buildings. The chapel is more enriched, and the exterior bears some resemblance in its general form to King's College in Cambridge. The corner turrets are less, and formed like those of King Henry the Seventh's Chapel at Westminster, but terminate with balls, instead of the rich fineals of the latter. The windows are beautiful, and the numerous buttresses surmounted with pinnacles give it an air of great lightness and elegance, which is enhanced by its commanding situation on the summit of the fine sloping lawn which descends to the river, and along which a terrace with embrasures contributes to the general effect of the whole.

The palace is formed by a line of irregular square masses of buildings, combining the character of the old English mansion with some features of the castellated style; several portions of which are rich with heraldic and other ornaments.

The principal apartments are distinguished by a character of plain and simple elegance, and derive great beauty from their loftiness. The breakfast-room contains portraits of Bishops Cosins, (a fine engraving of which is one of the illustrations to Surtees' Durham), Crewe, Butler, Barrington, and of the present venerable and munificent prelate. In an adjoining room is a painting of Niagara falls.

The dining-room is adorned with paintings of Jacob and the twelve Patriarchs,—the four Evangelists,—Cornaro by Titian, and of four Fathers. From thence the visitor is shewn to the drawing-room, a fine apartment, 62 feet long and 27 high. The furniture is appropriate and beautiful, and the floor is of oak. On the upper landing of the stair-case a window filled with plate glass from mullion to mullion, is so transparent that the stranger scarcely suspects it to be glazed, and fancies he feels the open air on approaching it. The prospect is beautiful.

The chapel, both exterior and interior, is the *lion* of the place. A handsome screen runs along near the west end of the interior, against which is a fine monument of Bishop Butler by Nollekins, 1775. The windows have been renewed, and the chapel ventilated with flues by the present bishop. Its great extent and loftiness have an imposing effect, which accords with the sentiments of devotion which the place is intended to inspire.

Following the Durham and Wolsingham turnpike, the brow of a hill commands a fine view of the latter town and of the fertile and well-wooded slopes of the vale, which stretch away to a considerable extent. The road winds pleasantly down the hill, and along the north side of the Wear to Wolsingham; the situation of which seems less beautiful on a near than on a distant inspection. It contains many good houses. The church is a plain and venerable-looking structure. The route continues westward through a somewhat less pleasing country; the vale is yet fertile and well wooded; but wants the luxuriance which is so much admired further down. The hills become more suddenly elevated, and bare green pastures and heathy moors increase. At Frosterly is a commanding eminence with a crushing-mill and washing places,—the first indications of mines which appear. The rocky bed of the river—the precipitous face of limestone quarries—the diminished verdure of the hills and their abrupt formation, now indicate the Geology of the Lead Measures, and gradually combine to form the characteristic features of a mining district.

Stanhope derives great beauty from the broad foliage which here adorns the vale. The opposite bank is studded over with trees, which give it a chequered and beautiful appearance. Some of them are ranged in hedge-rows, which have a formal appearance, while others are less regularly arranged in masses, of breadth and variety, much more interesting than the other portion. Their contrast affords a simple but useful lesson in ornamental planting, which the improved taste of the present day has discovered to be much more dependant on the freedom and simplicity of nature than the formal rules of art.

There are some fine walks by the water side. A walk to the foot of the rectory garden affords a limited but very beautiful view of Stanhope Castle and of the Rectory House, which stand on a fine terrace commanding the gardens below, in which are extensive green-houses with quadrant roofs, &c. The adjoining masses of wood are happily arranged, and there are some large trees in the gardens, which have a noble effect. The castellated residence of Cuthbert Rippon, Esq. M. P. is seen to great advantage, and forms a fine contrast to the dark umbrage behind. * Some very neat houses continue eastward along the same terrace, behind which, in the street, is a short avenue of lofty trees.

A small plain cross stands in the midst of the town, and near it is the Church, an ancient edifice. The living is one of the richest in the kingdom, being principally derived from the minerals in this extensive parish, and was recently held by that celebrated

---

* A mezzotinto engraving of this view, which gives an excellent idea of the scenery, has lately been executed by Mr. Collard, of Newcastle.

champion in political controversy, Dr. Philpotts, now Bishop of Exeter.

A steep hill on the north of Stanhope terminates in a heathy eminence of considerable height, which may be considered as the commencement of the barren and lofty ridges which crown the sides of the upper part of Weardale. Near the village of Eastgate the formation of the opposite banks resembles that of the banks of Tyne at Kirkhaugh in Northumberland, and historical associations contribute to strengthen the resemblance. The encampments of the Scottish army in Weardale, when opposed to Edward III., remain on the one, and on the other are still more observable traces of the Romans when encamped at Whitley Castle.

From Stanhope the traveller rapidly advances into the interior of the mining district; but many a pleasant spot beguiles the way, and many a hospitable home is to be found in this and the adjoining dales. Mr. Pearson, whose animated sketch of Teesdale has been quoted, (see page 145), spent some years in the adjacent vale of Nent, and, on leaving it, indulged a poetic vein at the expense of the severer features of the climate and scenery. But however uninviting to a stranger, the attractions of a native place are ever powerful in the human breast; and that such attractions are here to be found, may be readily conceived from Mr. Pearson's eulogium on the inhabitants.

> "Yet, ah! as I depart;
> The starting tears betray my anguished heart;
> For there are some that on these mountains dwell,
> Whose breasts with friendship's purest feeling swell,
> And though the clime I justly may condemn,
> Oh! my heart bleeds to bid farewell to them."

Continuing this route, cultivation at length skirts only the sides of the river, the mountains assume a huge massive character, and the prospect becomes wild and solitary. The road follows close by the side of a mountain stream, and by a long and tiresome ascent gains the summit of a lofty ridge, at which the tourist again enters the manor of Alston Moor.

The traveller now descends steeply over wastes of barren and dreary aspect to the mining village of Nent Head, which has been almost entirely rebuilt by the London Lead-Company, under the able management of Mr. Stagg. Here is a market-house with a clock tower, a Methodist chapel, a good inn, and very extensive washing-floors, where excellent arrangements are made for carrying on the various processes of washing the ore. Brigalburn Hush is in the immediate neighbourhood, and merits a visit from the geologist and from the lover of romantic scenery. The yawning aspect of the rocks, torn asunder by repeated torrents, is uncommonly imposing.

Continuing along the road to Alston, the tourist midway passes Nent Hall, a residence of John Wilson, Esq. of Shotley Hall, in the county of Northumberland, under the able management of whom, and of his son, Thomas Wilson, Esq., the mines of Hudgill Burn were productive of subterranean treasures almost unexampled in the annals of mining. The same skill and perseverance which won this store of wealth, have been unremittingly exercised in conducting the extensive works connected with it, and afford a convincing proof how much a judicious spirit of enterprise is calculated to promote the most important interests.

It has been very justly observed, that " a knowledge of our subterranean wealth would be the means of furnishing greater opulence to the country than the acquisition of the mines of Mexico and Peru ;" yet the several aids which science affords towards this

desirable object have never met with that attention in
England which foreigners so zealously bestow upon
them.   The subject, however, is now becoming more
understood, and it is reasonable to hope that many
advantages may at future periods be derived from
regular and methodical records of subterranean works,
and that, aided by such materials, philosophy may
unfold to geologists and miners such discoveries as may
tend to the more certain and successful prosecution
of adventures in the mineral world.   Hudgill-Burn
Mine stands forth as a memorable instance of judicious
and persevering enterprise, and its dazzling riches
gave a fresh impulse to mining in Alston Moor.   While
it has contributed an ample store to the funds of
Greenwich Hospital, its respectable proprietors also
have derived princely incomes from it ; and, as forming
one of the features of the society of these mining
districts, it ought not to be omitted that generous
hospitality and social worth have ever formed a bond
of union among the *Hudgill-Burn Masters,* to many of
whom the Author cannot but express his acknowledg-
ments for frequent permission to view the interior of
the mine, and for much personal kindness during his
residence in its vicinity.

On the broad expansive slope of the north-east
declivity of the mountain of Middle Fell, and about
half a mile west of Nent Hall, is the principal entrance
of Hudgill-Burn mine, and near it are the bing-steads,
washing-floors, and machinery of the establishment.
From thence the turnpike continues along the side of
the hill, and, at the distance of two miles, the traveller
reaches the town of Alston, and completes a tour of
some of the most interesting portions of the Northern
Mining Districts.

The dales of the rivers East and West Allen present

many interesting objects of attention, both in mining and in natural scenery; any detailed notices of which would exceed the limits of this work. From Allenheads a very excellent line of road has been formed to Allendale Town, preserving nearly a uniform level, while the old road followed a circuitous course over hill and dale of the most inconvenient steepness. From Allenheads this road is continued to Weardale, and the tourist, instead of re-entering Alston Moor, may continue down East Allendale, to join the Hexham and Alston turnpike near Cupula Bank, or may follow the more wild and romantic ride by Coalcleugh and West Allen as delineated on the map.

Such are a few of the principal features of the lead-mining regions of the North of England. The tourist who has visited the upper dales of Tyne, Wear, and Tees, will be able to form a tolerably correct idea of the mining districts; but there are many other detached mineral places throughout this portion of the kingdom which have many claims on the tourist's attention. From the lead-mines near Blanchland, a valley of most romantic scenery extends nearly to Newcastle; and, like the celebrated vale of Matlock, has a river *Derwent* flowing through the midst of it. This fine scenery will ere long be opened to more general observation, a new road being about to be made along the banks of the river, which will form an addition to the many picturesque roads of England, and at the same time open out an extensive and highly interesting district. Lead-mines are also spread over the range of the Penine Alps to a great extent; but the want of good roads and of concentrated objects of interest renders them unsuited as places for general observation. Buried in deep and romantic recesses among the mountains of the Cumbrian group, the tourist, in

R

traversing their wild and grand but solitary scenery, may find the miner pursuing his laborious searches for lead and copper. At Roughtengill and Silvergill the character of the landscape is truly alpine, and some of the approaches to the mines are perfectly terrific. Swaledale, in Yorkshire, is an interesting mining vale, and presents a great variety of scenery, from the luxuriance of fertile and woody lands to the lofty heath-clad mountains which crown the middle range of the chief mineral districts of the north. Of this valley an excellent description is given in the " Beauties of England and Wales," in the appendix to Yorkshire.

The lead-mines of Derbyshire also are situated in the midst of magnificent scenery, so that in the north of England, the mineral districts may be considered as comprising the most interesting and romantic portion of the island. From the brief notices here collected, which are for the greater part original, and have not before been offered to the public, it may be seen, that, considered as mineral districts, they not only afford most interesting subjects of attention in their mines and subterranean treasures, but also lead the tourist in those directions where nature assumes her wildest and most romantic forms—to the lofty mountain and expansive view—the rapid stream—the rolling cataract, and all the other majestic accompaniments of alpine scenery. Leaving these districts, towards the more level and expanded regions nearer to the coast, the traveller is led through valleys, whose umbrageous riches and deep seclusion afford the highest delight to a lover of nature. Whether as regards the importance of its mines and the accommodation of access to them, the goodness of the roads and constant communication from neighbouring towns, or the number and interest of its several objects of attention, the manor of Alston Moor holds a distinguished place in the mineral geography of the kingdom, and is consequently better adapted than others for popular description. Its antiquarian and various other attractions are comparatively unknown, and thousands have passed on either side of the mining districts, on their way to the mountains and lakes of Scotland, unconscious that nature, science, and art have combined to invest with peculiar interest the neglected, but grand and interesting scenery of the mining dales of the north of England.

A residence of four years in Alston Moor, and frequent opportunities of visiting the mines and scenery of this and neighbouring mining districts, afforded by extensive surface and mineral surveys, have left a vivid impression, which has not been effaced by subsequent visits to some of the most celebrated landscape scenery in the kingdom; nor less indelibly recorded on that page where every day the leaf is turned to read them, are a grateful remembrance and unfeigned esteem for many of the excellent inhabitants of the mining districts, whose genuine worth and hospitable kindness will be found one of the chief attractions by those who shall deem this hitherto neglected portion of the kingdom deserving of their attention.

FINIS.

Printed by W. DAVISON, *Alnwick.*

PUBLISHED BY

W. DAVISON, ALNWICK.

A PLAN OF THE MINING DISTRICT OF ALSTON
MOOR, with part of the Dales of Tyne, Wear, and Tees, and
the several new Lines of Road recently made in these Districts.
Drawn by T. SOPWITH, Land and Mine Surveyor. Price 1s.
6d. plain, or 2s. coloured.

THE HISTORY OF ALNWICK, ALNWICK CASTLE,
ABBEYS, &c., with numerous Engravings of Views, Plans,
Antiquities, &c. Price 10s. 6d. Demy 8vo, or 21s. Post 4to.

THE HISTORY AND ANTIQUITIES OF HEXHAM,
with Engravings. By A. B. WRIGHT. 1 vol. 8vo, 6s. 6d.